In the early days of the Second World War, the enemy had all but crippled the United States Navy Pacific Fleet's battleships. The Army was bravely fighting a losing battle in the Pacific. And in that darkest hour, America needed heroes more than ever. In April 1942, a brave group of pilots became those heroes, with just . . .

THIRTY SECONDS OVER TOKYO

"It leaves no doubt about the fighting, tough, quietly heroic qualities of U.S. fliers."

—*Time*

"It is a manly young American's simple, straightforward record of events and impressions gathered on one of the most desperate and colorful adventures of modern times."

—*New York Herald Tribune*

"[A] classic, well-written story of the Doolittle Raid."

—*Naval Aviation History*

"[A] taut, exciting work."

—*The Santa Fe New Mexican*

THIRTY SECONDS OVER TOKYO

CAPT. TED W. LAWSON

Edited by ROBERT CONSIDINE

POCKET STAR BOOKS

New York   London   Toronto   Sydney

A Pocket Star Book published by
POCKET BOOKS, a division of Simon & Schuster, Inc.
1230 Avenue of the Americas, New York, NY 10020

Copyright © 2002 by Ellen R. Lawson

Published by arrangement with Brassey's, Inc.

ISBN: 978-0-7434-7433-7

First Pocket Books printing August 2004

20 19

POCKET STAR BOOKS and colophon are registered
trademarks of Simon & Schuster, Inc.

Cover design by James Wang

Manufactured in the United States of America

For information regarding special discounts for bulk purchases,
please contact Simon & Schuster Special Sales at 1-800-456-6798
or business@simonandschuster.com.

Dedicated to

Lieutenants Bill Farrow, Dean Hallmark,
George Barr, Bob Hite, Bob Meder, Chase Nielson,
Sergeants Harold Spatz, William Dieter,
and Corporals Donald Fitzmaurice and
Jacob Deshazer.

They didn't get back. God help them.

Contents

Foreword

The events Ted Lawson describes in his classic wartime memoir occurred four months after Japanese naval forces struck U.S. forces and bases at Pearl Harbor, Hawaii, on December 7, 1941. This surprise attack not only killed more than 2,000 American servicemen and civilians but thrust the country into what had been a mostly European war, making the conflict truly a world war with the stakes nothing less than the survival of western civilization.

The first six months after Pearl Harbor were arguably the most trying period of America's 166-year existence. For the most part, the news from the Pacific was relentlessly bad. Island outposts, cities, and colonies fell to the Japanese as they steamrolled across Asia. Thousands of Americans, military and civilian, were prisoners, facing difficult times under captors whose values and heritage were completely different from their own. Although U.S. Navy carrier groups struck Japanese bases and islands in February and

March, these low-level raids were no more than pin pricks and did not result in any major advance for the Americans nor a defeat for the Japanese.

Something was desperately needed to bolster American home-front morale and to give a shot in the arm to the beleaguered soldiers, airmen, sailors, and Marines struggling to contain the new enemy's drive across the Pacific. Sound familiar?

Three months before the 60th anniversary of the Pearl Harbor attack, America was again struck by a murderous sneak attack, this time killing thousands of innocent civilians and their would-be rescuers in New York and nearly 300 civilians, service members, and peaceful travelers in Washington, D.C., and Pennsylvania. The results of these simultaneous raids on September 11, 2001, shattered long-held feelings of safety and relative isolation that Americans had enjoyed since the end of World War II. It was the same false feeling of security that had colored American impressions of the conflicts in Europe and China in 1940. It could also be said that seeing the actual events as they happened—the crash of two airliners into the World Trade Centers, or the fall of the towers—gave the true sense of disaster lacking in 1941.

The terrorist attacks of 2001, however, made the United States realize that it was no longer free from the shadow of mass destruction by people whose basic beliefs and attitudes conflicted with everything Americans had believed in for more than two centuries. Again, something had to be done to bolster flagging morale and relieve the shock. The initial reaction included a lengthy bombing campaign against terrorist home bases in Afghanistan.

In 1942, technological capabilities generated a surprise attack against the enemy's homeland, something he, too, in his own smugness, did not expect or fear. The results of the Doolittle raid were a definite boost to American morale, and a similar heightened fear in all circles of Japanese society that more attacks could and would come. Front-line fighter squadrons were recalled from the Pacific at a critical time to defend the homeland, and the military pushed planning and execution of the Midway operation ahead to a time when the Imperial Navy was not completely ready.

Older Americans who also lived through World War II can immediately recall where they were that terrible Sunday in early December when news of the Pearl Harbor attack blared from radios. Many of these senior citizens now say the events of September 11, 2001, are infinitely more powerful than those of December 7, 1941. Pearl Harbor was far away, and the targets were, for the most part, military. Also, having listened to the war news from Europe for more than two years, most Americans believed it was only a matter of time before they would be fighting, too.

The terrorist strikes 60 years later, however, were of such an unexpected and terrible nature that no one could have conceived their coming, even with other related activities ranging from attacks on Olympic athletes in 1972, to pleasure ships and American airliners in 1985, American military bases in war-torn Lebanon in 1983, and destruction of American embassies in Africa that killed native and American workers at random in 1998.

In 1942, standoff cruise missiles and electronically guided bombs were far in the future. The only way to hit back was to go to the enemy's front door. The calling card had to be hand-delivered by brave men stretching their personal and technological capabilities to their utmost. When this book and a subsequent feature movie appeared late in World War II, the tide of the war had already turned in the Allies' favor. But when the Doolittle Raiders flew their B-25s from the carrier *Hornet* across the Japanese homeland, the news electrified the nation and gave America its first glimmer of hope that things would improve.

Another similarity between these two milestone periods in American history was the role of the families who sent loved ones off to war, not knowing if they would ever see them again. The only major difference is that in 2001, the departing family member could very well be a woman—a wife, daughter, sister, or mother. In 1942, when Ted Lawson told his new wife, Ellen, goodby and that she would not hear from him for several months, each knew they would truly be out of contact with the other for a long time. Today, while the separations are as long, and the recent campaign potentially as dangerous, families keep in touch via e-mail and satellite-powered phones. But the time apart is no less harrowing for everyone.

Like their grandparents and their great-grandparents in 1942, today's young combatants and their families face the uncertainty of war and separation. And like the previous generation, they do so knowing their job is nothing less than the preservation of all they and their compatriots hold dear.

Besides the enthusiastic help of Mrs. Ellen R. Lawson, we would like to thank Mr. Robert Cressman of the Naval Historical Center, Mr. Hill Goodspeed of the National Museum of Naval Aviation, and Mr. Stan Cohen, publisher of Pictorial Histories Publishing Company for their aid in producing this special edition of this book.

Peter B. Mersky
April 2002

Preface

Two officers of the U. S. Army Air Force sat at a table in a Washington hotel, a few weeks after Pearl Harbor. One was a General—big, ruddy, tough and gray. The other was a Lieutenant Colonel—stocky, scrappy-looking, eager.

For two hours the Lieutenant Colonel spoke to the General and marked up the tablecloth. At first the General laughed mockingly at what the Lieutenant Colonel said. Then he listened. He pulled his chair closer to the table, and listened more intently.

Finally the General slapped the table resoundingly. "By God, it sounded crazy when you first mentioned it," he said, "but I think you can do it. I'll go to bat for you and help you get things lined up. It certainly would give the country a lift."

The Lieutenant Colonel leaned back in his chair and smiled with relief. Then he grinned from ear to ear when the General wagged a finger at him and warned:

"But listen here, damn you: as soon as you *do*

bomb Tokyo you get the hell back here to Washington and go to work!"

This, then, is the story of a man who helped carry out that mission.

Introduction

This story is true. I was a part of this adventure from the beginning and I am still involved. Ted Lawson and I met at Los Angeles City College. He was studying aeronautical engineering days and working nights in the drafting department at Douglas Aircraft. An instructor, Frank Trueblood, advised Ted that to advance his career he should join the Army Air Corps as a flying cadet. He was accepted and started his training in April 1940 at Hancock Field in Santa Maria, California. Then it was on to Texas, first Randolph Field then Kelly Field, where he received his diploma and wings, graduating with the Class 40G, on November 15, 1940.

Ted received orders to join the 17th Group, 95th Squadron, at McChord Field, Washington. He needed time in the service to decide whether he wanted a military career or to pursue drafting for an aviation company. We had become engaged that September, but I continued working in Los Angeles at Sears-Pico and kept in touch with Ted through letters. Because Ted's work required travel all over the country, he was never in one spot long enough for us to settle down.

We finally married on September 5, 1941. I took a late flight from Los Angeles to Portland, Oregon, changed planes for the leg to Spokane, Washington, where Ted and two of his buddies, Bob Gray and Frank Grubb, met me. The three of us drove the short distance across the border to Coeur d'Alene, Idaho. Ted and I obtained a marriage license from a sleepy courthouse clerk and, after locating the justice of the peace, were married just before midnight. Gray and Grubb were our bridesmaids.

Two days later, the 17th Group left for southern maneuvers in Jackson, Mississippi. Ted's mother, who had arrived in Spokane the day after we were married, and I started the trip back to Los Angeles in Ted's '39 Buick. We didn't expect to see Ted for three months, so again it was back to writing letters.

On December 5th, Ted arrived at March Field. With little warning, I barely had enough time to drive the 80 miles to meet him. We had a nice dinner and spent the night in Riverside. Next day, we visited his mother in Los Angeles and planned how to spend his month's leave. On Sunday morning, December 7th, we ate breakfast at the Pig 'n Whistle on Hollywood Boulevard. Coming out of the restaurant, we heard a radio blasting out the news that "Pearl Harbor had been attacked . . . all servicemen return to your bases at once." What a blow. We said goodbye to his mom and returned to March Field. We listened to Roosevelt's speech on the car radio before he flew back to Mc-Chord. Another goodbye.

As the holidays approached, the Army allowed wives to join their husbands at McChord. Ted and I checked into a nearby motel. Years later, the owner's young son recalled how Ted would sweep low over the motel as he left at 5 A.M. for submarine patrol and again when he returned. I recall that the Army allowed us to pick a small Christmas tree from those growing on the base. Driving through the wooded area Ted suddenly stopped, jumped out of the car with his arms over his head. An MP had his rifle raised. We had not heard the command to stop, but Ted saw him in the rearview mirror. Security was tight on the base.

On Christmas Eve, Ted made a forced landing, bombs still on board, at Ilwaco, Washington. I was beginning to learn what it was like to be married to an Army pilot. On New Year's Day the squadron moved to Pendleton Army Air Force Base, Oregon. Ted drove with me in the Buick. We enjoyed the beautiful scenery along the Columbia River. At Pendleton, the weather closed in. The guys griped, because they could not fly and didn't receive flight pay for almost a month, but for me it was great. We had a chance to ski, sight-see, and go to weekend dances on the base. I also searched for a place to live and felt lucky to find a room with the Brantley family, whose son had enlisted. The Brantleys continued to be our good friends the rest of their lives.

Ted and I again said goodbye when the squadron moved to Columbia, South Carolina. Ted said it would be all right for me to drive to Columbia Army Air Force Base. Patti Gilbert, another Air Corps wife, and I started out early from Barstow, California, on Route 66 in our separate cars. On a bridge just outside of town, guards ordered us to turn off our headlights until we turned east. There had been a shelling on the coast of Santa Barbara and a blackout was in effect. We decided to check in with our husbands when we crossed the Mississippi River. After so many miles we were tired and lonely. Grubb answered the phone at the VOQ [visiting officers' quarters] and told me to head south to Eglin Field, Florida, where Ted had been transferred. Patti and I parted.

When I was late in arriving, Ted flew over, searching for me. North of Montgomery, Alabama, a farmer had pulled over to the right side of the road, looked back, saw me coming, and drove right into my path. I skidded into his old car, enough to damage my right front wheel. He took off on a side road with a trail of dust behind him. I was able to drive back slowly to the small town where I had just bought gas. The mechanic straightened the wheel and put on the spare tire, but after driving a few miles the spare went flat. It was getting dark but another driver saw my flashlight and stopped. He said he would alert the station to send help. The only choice was to put the damaged tire back on. It was slow going to Montgomery. I checked into the Whitely Hotel and phoned Ted.

I arrived at Eglin the next day to learn that Ted had volunteered for a secret mission. He said that it would take him out of the country for three months. There would be no word from him. I could not contact him. Dot Greening and I decided to spend this period at Myrtle Beach. We rented a cabin on the beach. Ginny Hilger and her two-year-old daughter, Jeannie, soon joined us.

Time passed slowly. We listened to the radio and wrote letters to our friends and families. I wrote in a notebook for Ted, which I saved for his homecoming. The Army didn't disclose any details of the raid, mostly out of concern for the safety of the men still in China, but newspaper headlines told of the raid with B-25 bombers over Japan.

Ted's mother suffered a stroke in May 1942, so I returned home. Through the grapevine we had heard that some of Ted's group were being kept in China to fight with Chennault's Flying Tigers. On May 21st, Ted's mother received a letter from Jimmy Doolittle that said Ted had been wounded in action and was on his way home. Mayme's doctor recommended this letter be kept from her, so I didn't know about it until arriving in Los Angeles. Mrs. Lawson's left side was paralyzed and she couldn't speak. She begged me with her eyes to get her home from a nursing place. I made these arrangements.

Later, General Doolittle phoned to ask if I wanted to come to Washington, D.C., to be with Ted, who was recuperating at Walter Reed Army Hospital. When the general visited him in the hospital, Ted said that he wanted to regain his health and be fitted for a new leg before I saw him. Besides, he didn't think I should travel because I was pregnant. But Doolittle said a letter had already been sent and I was on my way. It didn't take me long to pack. I told Ted's mother most of the story before I left.

During Ted's recovery at Walter Reed, we made many lifelong friends. Jimmy Doolittle was one of the first. On his first visit, his message was to keep busy, mind and body. I still remember him saying, "If you

don't have any downs, you won't be able to have ups."
Benny Howard, a famous flyer who had lost a leg when
the propeller fell off his plane during a race, proved a
great friend and helped build Ted's morale. Many of
those from the 17th Group came to visit and exchange
stories, some of which Bob Considine put into the
book. I won't forget Hank Miller [later Rear Admiral].
When he came for a visit, Ted suggested I go for a walk
so the two of them could talk privately. I didn't understand Hank's connection to the raid at the time. Ted
had not seen Hank since flying off the *Hornet* on April
18, 1942, and they had so many secrets to exchange.
Years later, Hank invited us to lunch on board his command, the carrier USS *Hancock*.

As Ted regained his health, he asked me to bring
him a notebook. He wanted to start writing down what
had happened to him. He especially wanted the Americans to know how the Chinese, at great risk to themselves, had saved the lives of so many Raiders. He told a
neighbor who worked for a newspaper that he was looking for a writer to help him tell his story. The neighbor
introduced Bob Considine to Ted. Ted and Bob clicked
right away. Bob soon had some notes ready to show
Charles Colebaugh, the managing editor of *Collier's*.
Because the government had released no news of the
raid, Bob received permission to write the story but it

all had to be kept secret until the War Department released it.

Collier's obtained first serial rights, then King Features, Random House, and MGM became involved. No news of the raid was disclosed until a year later for fear of reprisals against the Chinese and missionaries who had helped them. Ted and Bob changed the real names of people and places in the book to help protect them.

At Ted's request, the State Department located Dr. Chen in China and brought him to the United States for medical training. We wanted to help pay for this education, but learned that this is one of the many services our country provides. Dr. Chen received orientation at Johns Hopkins Hospital, was introduced in Congress, and interned at Los Angeles General Hospital. After his return to China, he enlarged his father's hospital where they had saved Ted's life. Both missionary families and nurse Mary Andrews from Australia made it safely out of China. They all became our good friends.

Ted received lots of letters. I answered as many as I could. Ted was released from Walter Reed Hospital and assigned to a tour of duty to Santiago, Chile, for the War Department in May 1943. First, he spent three months at MGM Studios to help Dalton Trumbo with the script for the movie, which was not released until 1944. He also helped Sam Zimbalist, the producer, select the actors and provide photos of the raid that he had collected.

During this time I took the Berlitz course in Spanish and shopped for household furnishings as we expected to be in Santiago for three years. Before the end of the first year, Ted had to return to Walter Reed for more surgery. This is when Eleanor Roosevelt invited him to the White House, beginning a close friendship that lasted the rest of her life. That's another story.

Ted asked for a change in duty where he could feel more useful. He was sent to March Field for a while. He decided to retire in 1945.

Ted had a successful career in civilian life. We were blessed with three children and had more than 50 wonderful years together. I have kept in touch with my Doolittle Raiders family and as many of their offspring as I can find. Random House published the Landmark edition of *Thirty Seconds over Tokyo* 10 years after the original edition. This version was edited slightly for the younger generation and became a "Book of the Month" selection. It became popular as a book report. Many students wrote to Ted that it was the first book they read, asking, "What else have you written?" These letters continued for years, making it all worthwhile.

This commemorative edition appears for the 60th anniversary of the raid. With the aftermath of the terrorist attacks on September 11, 2001, I hope that the generations of Americans that followed our World War II generation, who recall how that momentous event forever changed our world, will find something they can take with them as we move forward in the new century, trying to live our lives and raise our families during this world-wide struggle against alien forces.

                                          Ellen R. Lawson

THIRTY
SECONDS
OVER
TOKYO

I helped bomb Tokyo on the Doolittle raid of April 18, 1942. I crashed in the China Sea. I learned the full, deep meaning of the term "United Nations" from men and women whose language I couldn't speak. I watched a buddy of mine saw off my left leg. And finally I got home to my wife after being flown, shipped and carried around the world.

Now I'm in line for the aeronautical engineering research job which I wanted in the first place.

That's the story, briefly. Maybe the cards would have dealt out that job to me if I hadn't volunteered for the raid on Japan. Maybe not. I don't really have regrets, now. At first it was a little tough. People in little villages in China, in New Delhi and in Washington would look at me and feel sorry for me. And I'd have to curse or think hard about something else to keep from blubbering like a damned kid.

Now it's all right. I was one of the first of the badly wounded to get back to Washington. I guess I was a little hard to believe. One day I was crutching down a long corridor in the War Department when an elderly lady, a clerk, stopped me. She looked me up and down, examined my service ribbons, stepped back and said, "Why, what can you do in the Army?"

Even a month or two before this happened, it would have hurt badly. But now I could get a little fun out of it. I told her I was a Western Union boy and would have to be getting along.

I guess my story starts with Ellen. Ellen is my wife. She's twenty-two, three years younger than I am. Ellen was never very far from my mind during this whole thing. I would have drowned right after the crash, if the memory of her had not made me struggle out of the seat I was strapped to. And I guess I would have given up later on, if Ellen hadn't been so swell about my leg and face.

I didn't know Ellen's name for a long time after I met her. Ellen was the librarian of Los Angeles Junior College. She used to let me sleep in the library. I was always sleepy. I worked at the Douglas plant eight hours at night and went to school eight hours during the day. Ellen would let me sleep for ten or fifteen minutes, between classes, wake me up and I'd go out to class, stretching. That was 1937 and 1938, when I was studying aeronautical engineering.

One day I was at my mother's house, and there was Ellen, just a couple of doors away, tossing a football to some neighbor's kids. I walked out and she tossed one to me. We got to talking. You know how it is: you meet a slight acquaintance in some unexpected setting, and suddenly you're old pals.

I had to quit school about that time. It got too tough, trying to study and work at the same time. I was doing better at Douglas. I had gone beyond ordinary shop work—wiring engine nacelles and installing hydraulic tubing in B-18's. I had been put to work on the B-19.

The B-19 is still the biggest land plane ever built. It has never amounted to much because it can't go very fast. But it was all that most of us ever thought about when it was coming along, behind the big screens Douglas set up in front of it. As things turned out, they let me design the landing flaps, for braking the big crate, and the cowl flaps, for regulating the flow of air around the four motors. And, of course, the hydraulic system that operated them. I was getting ahead.

I've always been hungry to learn everything about planes. That was what was in my head that day in Minneapolis, a couple of years later, when I volunteered for the "dangerous, important, interesting" mission which turned out to be the Tokyo raid.

It was that curiosity about planes, and an interest in learning more than the blueprint side of the business, that put me in a civilian flying school and made me join the Army as a flying cadet. My mother raised Cain when I did that and, from a lot of standpoints, she was right. I was chucking a $36-a-week job with a company that was beginning to get big war orders from abroad for a $75-a-month job that might break my neck. But I wanted experience. I wanted to get my fingers into different kinds of planes and see how they worked. The Army had those planes, and Ellen saw it my way, even after Douglas said they'd give me a good raise if I stayed. You see, we wanted to get married. But now we'd have to wait at least until after I had gotten my wings.

The reason I tell you this, about enlisting, is that some people have been nice enough to think that I did it because I had chosen the right cause and was getting ready early to fight for it. But there didn't seem to be much likelihood that we'd get into the war when I enlisted early in 1940. It was more or less selfish on my part, I guess. I wanted the knowledge about planes that the Army could teach me.

About the only eventful thing about my training at Randolph and Kelly Fields—aside from what seemed like a Utopia of interesting engineering courses—was that one day I came out of a dive too late and shaved a sorghum patch right down to the skin. I got my wings on November 15, 1940.

That training period did something to me spiritually. It gave me my first real feeling of belonging to something; of being proud of being a part of a team. Graduating there is something like June Week, I guess. The outgoing class, after treating the younger men like dogs for a long time, suddenly is overwhelmed with brotherly love. We call it "Recognition Day." It's a nice tradition. From that day on I knew that, for me, there would now be more than just *taking* something the Army was offering. I'd want to be *giving*, too.

My first week out of Kelly was hell. Six members of my class were killed that week on the way to assigned posts. I had been at the wedding of two of them, married right after graduation ceremonies. It was an awful shock. I felt that in seven days I matured about seven years.

At Kelly the instructors decided that I was too tall for pursuit ships and more suited physically and temperamentally for bombers. That was all right. So was the fact that they seemed to think more of me as a pilot than as an engineer.

I knew that some day I'd get to do the thing I wanted to do and knew best. In the meantime I was eager for the experience.

I was sent to McChord Field, near Tacoma, and Uncle Sam began paying me $245 a month on account of my gold bars. At McChord I went into B-18's, the kind I helped to build at Douglas, and then checked out in the improved B-23. By February of 1941, I was a first pilot.

Two months later, after a lot of wild speculation, seven new B-25's were sent to McChord and I couldn't eat until I had a crack at mine. I would have slept in it that night if they would have let me. Our bunch, the Seventeenth Group, was the first to get B-25's. You just had to stand there and look at them, and breathe heavily. We were learning a lot from the war abroad. The B-25 proved that at first sight. My hands itched to unroll the blueprints on this job. The work that must have gone into it—from the bottom of its tricky tri-cycle landing gear to the tip of its double rudders high in back!

I saw a lot of the B-25's after that. I flew a succession of them as they went through their growing pains. Maybe I helped shake a few "bugs" out of the first model. It's a grand ship, fast, hard-hitting and full of fight. God knows that the last one I ever flew—it was the best—deserves a better fate than it found. What is left of it is on exhibition in Tokyo today.

Our first B-25's came to us virtually untried. That

made our test flights so much more interesting. We flew them across the country to Langley Field, Virginia, and never spared their feelings. We tested their speed, firepower, gas consumption, ability to take rough handling and bomb capacity. I dropped a 2,000-pounder near Langley one day that had the citizens pretty indignant, even though it had been advertised in the newspapers three days in advance.

The main trouble with the first B-25's was that the ship was so fast that the slipstream kept the rear gunner from giving us much real protection. His single 50-calibre machine gun wasn't operated from a power-driven turret. The barrel just stuck out. The next model put the gunner in cramped quarters at the extreme end of the fuselage, still with one 50-calibre gun. But the third model we got—the type we used on the Japanese raid—placed the rear gunner under a power-driven plastic turret about three-quarters of the way to the end of the fuselage. And gave him two 50-calibre stingers.

War was a part of our every thought as we came up to the Autumn of 1941. I felt that the world had shrunk like a prune. A group of Russian aviators barged into McChord one night, and I followed them around like a kid, thinking to myself that here we all were, just about in the same fight together, yet as distantly removed in almost everything as men of Earth and men of Mars.

But we had one meeting ground that needed no interpreter—those B-25's. They loved them as much as we did. You could see it in their faces and hear the tone of it in their jabbering.

A lot of things were happening that I wanted to share with Ellen. I missed her. You see, by now we had decided that we'd wait until I was taken into the regular Air Force (I was still in the Reserve) before we got married. But during the first week in September, 1941, I found out that the squadron was going off on a long maneuver that would involve a lot of bombing and night flying. Anything can happen on those things—and did—so when I learned about the assignment, I called Ellen on the long-distance phone and told her what I was thinking.

Ellen flew up from Los Angeles to Spokane, where I went to meet her. We were married late that night. That was September 5th. We took Bob Gray and Frank Grubb, my classmates at Kelly, to stand up for us. We drove to a place named Coeur d'Alene, Idaho, about thirty miles from Spokane, made a lot of noise and got a justice of the peace out of bed. He opened up the courthouse for us, near midnight, flashing his torch around the dark place, looking for a light switch. It was a real nice wedding. It didn't seem very important to either of us that marriage forfeited my chances for a regular commission. A reserve status looked good enough then.

Two days later our bunch took off for Jackson, Mississippi, and by the night of September 8th we were in the midst of a sham battle that rarely got around to being sham. That night Lieutenant Davey Jones, who was later to become an important member of the Japanese trip, broke us in on night-formation flying and gave us all a scare by slipping now and then to within a few feet of our wing tips. We were going to see a lot of Davey before we were through.

The maneuvers were close to the real McCoy. We were on alert twenty-four hours a day. Other bombing squadrons would come over, night or day, and litter our hangars with sacks of flour, while our fighting planes buzzed around them. We tried to bomb Shreveport before the P-38's and P-39's could intercept us. We worked and sometimes slept in steel helmets, and carried .45's. General Arnold was on hand, working harder than the rest of us and sore as hell every time the "umpire" failed to give us the nod.

I got a little time off, but it wasn't relaxing. My plane needed repairs, so I flew it to Patterson Field, Dayton, then on to Washington. Secretary of War Stimson was at Bolling Field when I put it down. He told me that the Government had offered the Russian aviators their choice of ten U. S. multi-motored planes, under Lend-Lease. The Russian General at his side, he explained, liked the B-25 but wanted to give it one more test.

The Russian General, an interpreter, Lieutenant Bailey and I got back in the plane. The General asked us—or told us—that he was going to take the controls just after we got off the ground. He wasn't kidding. He took us for a ride I'll never forget. When we were just a few feet off the ground he banked the ship and laid it over at a 90-degree angle. I was a passenger, standing up, but with the side window just in front of my face. The General insisted on staying right over the city of Washington, and not very high, while he gave that B-25 a test that would frighten a test pilot. He was a wild man, that General, but one hell of a flier.

Back at Jackson, Bob Gray was nearly killed. And nearly took me with him. The B-25 he was using that day had a bad left-wheel brake. I landed just ahead of him, rolled to the end of the runway and turned off to the right. I braked my ship and stopped, for there wasn't any more room for me to roll, and Bob was coming in. I was cornered.

As soon as Bob put the brakes on, his plane swerved toward my parked job, because only his right wheel was slowing down. So he revved his right engine and that straightened him out on the runway again. Then he braked again, and once more he headed for me. Then he revved the right engine again.

It was a good idea, but those B-25's like to roll on forever. He was rolling much too fast to turn to the left, for that would have rolled off his tires and tipped him over. Finally his right tire blew out from the uneven pressure put on it. The B-25 swung around, just short of my hemmed-in plane, and simply fell to pieces. You should have seen those fellows pouring out of it!

It was close, but just not our turn. Bob went on to Japan, got through that one all right, and then was killed in India. He was a fine pilot and a wonderful guy. If he had to go, I hope it was a bad crash. I mean I hope there was nothing lingering about it. The very bad ones are the best for the men. I know.

Lieutenant Butler, another man from our class, wasn't as lucky on those maneuvers. He was killed near the end of the tests. His B-25 went into a "slow roll" while taking off the short Augusta, Georgia, field. Its 100 octane went all over the place and ignited. There wasn't much left of anyone or anything by the time the ambulance and fire apparatus reached it. The same apparatus came out after me at Augusta, twice. There was a broad ditch at the end of the runway. I used to run the length of the runway on the take-off, duck the nose of my B-25 down in the ditch for extra speed, and then go up. The boys thought I was crashing, and I got a bawling out for it.

Those maneuvers were rougher than a cob. We worked with and against tanks, with and against truck concentrations. We bombed and got bombed. I had a left brake go bad on a landing and got out of it by Gray's method of braking and revving, braking and revving. We flew endlessly on observation work, spotting distant objects, and we had to bring back the right reports. About the only relief we got was the night in Augusta when one of the boys was turned down by a lady cashier when he tried to cash a check. He made some remark about the South, got slapped by the cashier and was tossed into the local clink. Before morning a lot of his friends were in there—the result of trying to get him out without bail.

It was December 6th when we got back to the West Coast. We were supposed to slip in before defending P-38's could spot us, and we did. But Ellen was a little more alert. She was there at March Field waiting for me. We had been married three months and together only two days. I had a leave coming and sure needed it.

Ellen and I were walking out of the Pig 'n Whistle, on Hollywood Boulevard, the next morning after breakfast, when we heard about Pearl Harbor. There was a radio on a news-stand. We just stood there with the other people, listening to the first bulletins. The Japs! I couldn't figure it at first. What about that Peace Envoy—what's his name? How the devil did they get bombers as far east as Hawaii?

I looked at Ellen and we walked away from there. I told her how strange it seemed to me, after thinking only about the Germans for so long. I told her that every bomb we had dropped, real or flour-sack, every real or blank machine-gun bullet we had fired, every scouting trip, every maneuver for weeks and weeks had been directed at the vision of one opponent—Germany. Every plane I dreamed of fighting was a Messerschmitt. Now Japan!

I had to get to March Field as quickly as I could. Ellen had my car, so we drove by my mother's house, said good-bye, and then drove the eighty miles to March Field in eighty minutes.

I was in the war. There were times during those months of maneuvers when I asked myself what the hell I was doing there, risking my neck when the thing I wanted in the Army was research work. Once I even made formal application through the proper channels for a transfer to that branch of the Air Force. But it was slow going, that way. Now, as Ellen and I drove up to

March Field, we were stopped by sentries and felt the tension around the place, and I was glad the Army had taught me how to fight. There would be plenty of time for the other. Now I wanted the feel of that B-25 in my hands—not a blueprint. I didn't feel heroic. I just felt ready, and thanked God I was.

Our planes had already been dispersed all over March Field. I reported and was told that we had been ordered to the new field the Army was then still building at Pendleton, Oregon. But the time of our take-off was postponed until the next day.

That next morning Ellen and I sat in our car, turned on the radio and listened to the President. The wives of some of the other fellows had driven out to the field, too. Looking around us, Ellen and I could see them listening in their cars. We didn't say much during the Declaration of War.

When the President finished, Ellen said, "I'm going to drive the car up to Pendleton and live there."

I said no. I had been there, and the living conditions were tough. So, after a short time, I was kissing Ellen good-bye. The squadron took off and flew to San Francisco, and then on to Pendleton. We came in at ten o'clock that night and landed on snow-covered runways. It was eighteen below zero. And tough. A mental shock. Peace . . . The start of a leave . . . Being with

Ellen in the sunshine of Hollywood . . . Then war . . . Work . . . More separation, and the sharp ice of the field cutting at my ankles as I ran for the Pendleton barracks.

One of the worst feelings about that time was that there was no tangible enemy. It was like being slugged with a single punch in a dark room, and having no way of knowing where to slug back. There was also the sobering thought that the same Japanese aircraft carriers which must have brought the bombers and certainly brought the fighters and torpedo planes to Hawaii might even now be on the way to our Coast. And, too, there was a helpless, filled-up, want-to-do-something feeling that they *weren't* coming—that we'd have to go all the way over there to punch back and get even.

That's the way it turned out.

In the middle of December, some of us were ordered back to McChord for submarine patrol work. Nobody wanted that assignment more than I did. I had tried it a few days before, after loading up with bombs at Seattle, and had made a mess of it—though it really wasn't my fault.

I was headed back for the field with my bombs, this day I speak of, when I got radio orders to drop them in the ocean before coming in. I had not sighted anything. When the word came to salvo the bombs I figured I might as well give the bombardier a little practice. So I made a run over a certain spot in the water and we dropped one. Then I swung around and let him take cracks with the rest of the bombs at the disturbance in the water caused by the first bomb.

The trouble was that I wasn't far enough off shore. Some people heard us, saw us making those runs, and there was a sub scare along that section of the coast. Later on I got the blame.

But that was all right. The important thing was that I was getting another chance at sub patrol and that I was going to be stationed close enough to the conveniences of Tacoma so that Ellen could come up for Christmas. We had now seen each other four days out of 106.

Ellen got to Tacoma late on the night of December 23rd. The next morning we got up very early and drove out in the country, looking for a Christmas tree small enough to get into a hotel room. We found one just in time to get it back to town and for me to get out to Mc-Chord and go to work. Brick Holstrom, who later made the Tokyo trip, Lieutenant Whitty and I took off and fanned out on three tangents where the Columbia River opens into the ocean.

Brick got a Jap sub that day. We saw him circling and dropping his bombs and, by the time we got over to where he was, the oil was coming up in greasy bubbles, as if some awful thing was throwing up under water. The sinking was confirmed.

The weather closed in on us right after that, and Brick, his bombs gone, headed back for land. I was wild to get a sub. So I dropped lower and lower under the weather, thinned down the gas mixture and decided I'd stay out there just as long as I could. Whitty had the same idea.

The weather reports were slow coming through that day. There was a radio silence, except for code transmission. That was slow, and bad news. McChord was closed solid. Tacoma was closed. So were Everett and Portland. Seattle was closing fast. Holstrom was the last plane in there.

Whitty and I stayed out. There wasn't much else we could do, and there was always a chance that we'd spot something. But gasoline, as I was to find out on the Tokyo trip, hasn't got a heart. Whitty finally made a run for land, and I found out later that he came down on a beach along the southern edge of Washington.

I got halfway to Portland when the gas needles began knocking against the peg. I looked in on a Navy field, but it was under construction and just a big mud cake. I had to get down now, and I wasn't going to unload those bombs. I went over the maps again and found a little emergency field at a place named Ilwaco, Washington. I remember repeating the vital statistics of the field and city. They were depressing: a 1,500-foot field, no runway, population 300.

The gas held out just long enough for me to find Ilwaco, circle the field three times and decide how I was going to set down our touchy load. We had 300-pounders with us.

The only thing to do was to land like the Navy: a ker-plunk, but just enough of a ker-plunk to slow it down a little and not enough to break anything. So on the third time around the field I put the three wheels down on a concrete road and we went like a bat out of hell across a little ditch, onto the field and splashed through three big shallow puddles that should have rolled us over, but didn't.

The mud was just about right. It slowed us down but didn't crack our nose wheel. We stopped in good time, but then the wheels began sinking into the mud, and the props, still spinning, churned into the stuff and buckled. We got out and it made me sick to look at the plane. I had only eighteen hours on it, and now it looked hopeless.

Ellen trimmed the tree that night and waited. I

guess it was tough on her, but finally one of the boys back at the field got in touch with her and told her I was okay. I had Christmas dinner the next day with an Ilwaco lumberman. He was real kind, but I kept thinking about Ellen and how we had planned to be together for our first Christmas—and how something always seemed to pull us apart.

Back at McChord we soon got some news that excited all of us. Our Squadron was ordered to Columbia, South Carolina, by way of Minneapolis, for patrol work against the German subs which were then sinking so many tankers off the Atlantic coast. Once again it was good-bye for Ellen and me.

My left engine quit and forced me down on a golf course at Rawlings, Wyoming. Later, continuing East, between North Platte and Omaha, I picked up a heavy load of ice and had to get down in a hurry once again. I got back to North Platte, nearly put it down in the snow on a golf course, then saw a little air field near by.

She went into that little field with so much class that it made your heart jump. It was a strange feeling, rolling across the snow at 90 or 100, taking off every time we hit a bump under the snow. It was the best landing I ever made, or, now, ever will. But it was the B-25 more than I. It was things like this that made me love that ship. It helps itself more than any plane I ever worked on or flew. It is so much more than an inanimate mass of material, intricately geared and wired and riveted into a tight package. It's a good, trustworthy friend.

When the weather would let us, we flew on to Minneapolis. There we had a sixty-gallon gas tank installed in each of the planes, ostensibly for submarine-patrol work over the Atlantic. We'd need those tanks, I said to myself. And I tried to picture what it would be like, out over the Atlantic. I prayed that I'd get a sub. Curiously, another gas tank was presently installed in our bomb bay.

I didn't know that the whole bewildering machinery of the raid on Japan was already beginning to function in Washington, along the Pacific Coast, Honolulu, China, and God knows where else. I didn't know that the extra tanks had nothing to do with subs.

The job of putting in the new tanks and checking over the planes was just about done. I was anxious to get going for Columbia and sub work. So it was a relief when I heard that Davey Jones, who had been in Dayton for a couple of days with our squadron commander, Captain Edward J. York, of San Antonio, Texas, wanted to see all officers in his hotel suite. We were staying in downtown Minneapolis. This, I figured, would be the notice of our clearance for Columbia.

We all strolled into the big hotel suite—there were twenty-four of us—and sat around on the beds and chairs, smoking and clowning a little. Most of us forgot to look at Davey very closely.

When we were all there, Davey went around and closed the doors of the suite. When he finally spoke, he didn't raise his voice.

"I've just come back from talking with Captain York," Davey said, quietly. "There's been a change. We're not going to work out of Columbia. Captain York wanted me to talk to you and see how many of you would volunteer for a special mission. It's dangerous, important and interesting," he added, after a pause.

One of the fellows spoke up and asked, "Well, what is it?"

"I can't tell you," Davey said. "I don't even know myself. I've got a hunch, but no real information, and I'm not talking about my hunch. All I can tell you is that it's dangerous and that it'll take you out of the country for maybe two or three months."

"Where?" somebody asked.

"I'm sorry I can't tell you any more," Davey said. "You've heard all the particulars I can give you. Now, who'll volunteer? It's perfectly all right if you don't. It's strictly up to you."

All of us volunteered.

The meeting broke up and we wandered off in small groups. Some of us went downstairs and had a drink and talked a long time about what had happened. We were still going to Columbia, Davey told us before we broke up, and we'd get our orders from there. We tried to figure out something from his sketchy outline, but it was hard. One of the fellows finally got it in his mind that we were going to South America, for sub-patrol work there, and that seemed to make as much sense as anything.

When the B-25's were ready—there were twelve or fifteen at Minneapolis—we flew down to Columbia. We hadn't heard another word about the mission we had volunteered for, and you know how your mind and imagination begin to work if you live with something like that for a while.

I took on a new crew at Columbia. I had come across the country with Lieutenant Dean Davenport, of Portland, Oregon, as my co-pilot. I liked the way he flew. At Columbia we added Lieutenants Charles L. McClure, of University City, Missouri, as navigator, and Bob Clever, of Portland, as bombardier. Our gunner-engineer became Corporal David Thatcher, of Billings, Montana. He was only nineteen, but very quiet and industrious. I had known all of them at Pendleton. McClure, Clever and Thatcher had come across the country to Columbia by a different route from the one Davenport and I had used. But it surprised us to find that they, too, had been approached and had volunteered for the secret mission. They didn't know any more about it than we did.

Without realizing it, I had picked my crew for the Tokyo trip.

We were at Columbia until near the end of February, 1942, testing and giving the ship its fifty-hour check, and by that time we were all jumpy. We knew that something big was happening, and that we would be in the middle of it, but we never heard a word.

Then we were ordered to fly to Eglin Field, near Pensacola. Our crew talked a lot about that on the trip down and came to a lot of haphazard conclusions. We certainly weren't going to fly to any foreign country from Eglin, we decided. We also decided that this would be where we'd train for whatever we were going to do and that "it" had something to do with flying over water—for Eglin is near the Gulf.

Our squadron put its three-prong wheels down on Eglin on February 28th. As I taxied across the field after the landing, I looked around and saw we had company. B-25's from three more squadrons of the 17th Group were scattered around the place. There were twenty-four bombers in all.

They must know something, I figured, but after I had checked in and talked to some of the boys in the other squadrons I found that they were as much in the dark as we were.

So that night we sat around and buffaloed about a lot of things, mostly guessing at what was in store for us. I remember one thing that was said early in the bull session. One of the boys from another squadron said to me, "Guess who's here?"

I said I couldn't guess.

"Jimmy Doolittle," he said. "He's a Lieutenant Colonel now, and I think he's going to have a hell of a lot to say about this mission."

We met Doolittle the next day, March 1st. I had heard and read a lot about him, of course, and had seen his picture a number of times. But it was quite a shock to see how young-looking his face was after those years of stunting, barnstorming and racing.

About 140 of us crowded into Eglin's Operations Office. We sat on benches and window sills and, when we were more or less quiet, Doolittle began to talk.

The first thing he said was, "If you men have any idea that this isn't the most dangerous thing you've ever been on, don't even start this training period. You can drop out now. There isn't much sense wasting time and money training men who aren't going through with this thing. It's perfectly all right for any of you to drop out."

A couple of the boys spoke up together and asked Doolittle if he could give them any information about the mission. You could hear a pin drop.

"No, I can't—just now," Doolittle said. "But you'll begin to get an idea of what it's all about the longer we're down here training for it. Now, there's one important thing I want to stress. This whole thing must be kept secret. I don't even want you to tell your wives, no matter what you see, or are asked to do, down here. If you've guessed where we're going, don't even talk about your guess. That means every one of you. Don't even talk among yourselves about this thing. Now, does anybody want to drop out?"

Nobody dropped out. Doolittle talked about ten more minutes without telling us anything more. It wasn't a pep talk, exactly, but when he finished I felt very impressed. We walked out quietly, not saying much.

Our orders were to get our ships in the air right away and spot the various auxiliary fields near Eglin. We did that most of the first day, keeping our traps shut. But that night, back in barracks, it was tough to stay away from the subject. It helped a little to play Hearts. When I got tired of that I got out the record player I had brought with me in the plane and our bunch sat around listening to "Chattanooga Choo Choo" and "Deep in the Heart of Texas" until we darn near wore them out. At least it kept us from thinking.

Ellen came in the next day. She had driven from Los Angeles to Columbia, and then had to drive to Eglin. She was tuckered out, but I hardly had time to talk to her. There was another meeting at just that time with Doolittle.

When we were all assembled in the Operations Office again, Doolittle gave us a sample of how secret the thing was. A couple of high-ranking Army officers happened to walk through the section of the Operations Office after Doolittle had started to speak, and he immediately stopped talking. I figured that whatever this thing was, there wasn't any fooling about it.

"The reason I want you to keep this thing secret is because if you start talking about it and the news or rumors get around, it'll endanger the lives of many others," Doolittle told us. "Your lives aren't the only ones at stake in this thing. There are a lot of people working on this mission. One slip could kill the whole thing.

"Has anybody tried to talk to you about this?" he asked us. "I mean anybody around the field?" There was no answer, so he continued, "Well, if anybody does approach you, get his name and I'll turn him over to the F.B.I.

"That's about the main thing I wanted to talk to you about," he finished. "But I can tell you this much: one of the most important parts of this training period will be practicing quick take-offs."

We got into the swing of things on the third day at Eglin. I fixed Ellen up in a hotel at Fort Walton, about twelve miles from the Field, and hardly ever saw her. Our planes were in the air at 7 A.M. each morning and sometimes we'd still be at it at 10 P.M. We got so much night flying at the start that I decided that the mission would be a night job, and it would have been if things had gone the way they were planned. I didn't have to be very smart to deduce that. They gave us live bombs one night and we dropped them on a burning target.

Doolittle wanted to keep us as close together as possible, so he arranged for us to take over an old hotel a mile and a half from the field. We called it the Officers' Club, and one by one the wives of the fellows drifted in and settled down. I moved Ellen in from Fort Walton.

The officers in charge were always keeping after us to see that our ships were in tip-top shape. We had to be sure the life raft worked. We had to check and recheck our instruments. We had to swing our compasses, for we had been warned that our mission would entail tricky navigation. Lifebuoys were placed three miles apart, out in the Gulf, and we had to make many speed runs over them to test our air-speed indicators.

Navigators had to learn the work of bombardiers. Pilots and co-pilots had to practice every job in the plane. One day we had to check the extra gas in the ship to test it for possible leaks. An extremely close record had to be kept of our gas consumption.

One morning I came out to my plane and found that somebody had chalked the words "Ruptured Duck" on the side of the fuselage. I grabbed Corporal Lovelace, a gunner I knew, and asked him to paint some sort of design on the ship. He's a good caricaturist. Lovelace got out his stuff and painted a funny Donald Duck, with a head-set and the earphone cords all twisted around his head.

Lovelace did a swell job in blue, yellow, white and red. Then he added something that gave all of us another laugh. Under Donald Duck he drew a couple of crossed crutches.

The other boys now got busy with insignias. In a couple of days a lot of hitherto anonymous B-25's took on such names as Hari Kari-er (a hefty hunch), Whiskey Pete, Anger Angel, Whirling Dervish, Fickle

Finger of Fate and one fellow painted the chemical formula for TNT on the side of his ship.

Take-off practice started the end of the first week at Eglin. One morning Doolittle introduced us to a Lieutenant, Senior Grade, of the Navy—Lieutenant Henry L. Miller. He had come over from Pensacola and would be our special instructor in quick take-offs. The Navy knew a lot about such things.

This practicing was done at auxiliary fields away from all eyes. Flags were placed along the white-lined runways of these fields at 200, 300 and 500 feet. The idea, we soon found out, was to get into the air in less space and time than we believed was possible for a B-25. We did this by dropping our landing flaps and pouring all the coal we could on the engines.

The mission for which we had all blindly volunteered took on shape and substance as the days passed. That we would be carted somewhere by the Navy was apparent after Lieutenant Miller lectured to us at great length on Navy courtesy and etiquette. He told us about saluting the national ensign on the stern of the ship we boarded, and gave us a glossary of nautical terms. He even told us how to take a shower bath on a ship without wasting water.

The bombing, wherever, whatever, whenever it would be, would be made from a low altitude. We learned this about ten days after we got to Eglin when we were told that the bottom gun-turret would be taken off our ships. That lightened each ship 600 pounds. Into the empty space was placed a bullet-proof forty-gallon gas tank.

Two reasons were given for the subsequent removal of the Norden bomb sight from all the ships. The first reason was sobering. "It's inevitable that some of the ships will fall in the enemy's hands," Doolittle told us. The second reason was understood immediately by all the bombardiers. The Norden bomb sight was not practicable at the heights at which we were bombing.

Captain Charles R. Greening designed the bomb sight that was now placed in our ships. Later there was a lot of talk about our "twenty-cent bomb sights." I guess it cost a little more than that, but it was fine for the things we had in mind. It was as simple as pointing a rifle at the object to be bombed and letting the bomb go when you had a bead.

This was the first time any of us had been called on to drop bombs from very low altitudes. The Ruptured Duck laid one of its 100-pound eggs in practice one day from 500 feet. The shock of the explosion on the ground threw me against the roof of the pilot's compartment and raised an egg on my head.

That bump didn't seem very important after we learned that on the mission we would use 500-pound bombs. Then I began to wonder whether dropping them would be suicide. We learned about the 500-pounders from a Colonel in Ordnance. He was flown to Eglin to speak to us on bombs. He took great delight in letting us know that instead of the usual charge of 35%, he was making up the special 500-pounders with a 50% charge. A confirmed report that we would bomb whatever we were going to bomb from 1,500 feet relieved the tension somewhat.

Doolittle, who was making frequent trips to Washington—apparently not trusting the telephone or telegraph wires—gave us another chance to back out about this time. One of the fellows did. The low-level bombing and souped-up take-offs were getting him down. The rest of us stayed on, and saw our ships' wings fitted with ice boots the next day.

It was all a part of the almost mystic ramifications of the mission which, in full flower, was perhaps the most intricately schemed, diligently practiced and far-flung military raid in history.

We had our only crack-up of the training period about March 15th. Lieutenant Miller, the Navy man, was in it. He was flying with Lieutenant Dick Joyce of Lincoln, Nebraska, with a load of dummy bombs and a full gas load, including the reserve tanks. It was during one of those hard-to-believe take-offs. Joyce got the wheels off the ground and pulled them up in a hurry, but the ship wobbled and dropped back on the runway. It skidded along, shrieking, on its belly; the props, which only have a nine-inch ground clearance, chewing themselves to pieces. We held our breath, waiting for the flames. But they didn't come.

It was just a part of our education. Soon all of us were able to get our fully loaded ships off the runway at between 55 and 60 mph with full flaps, whereas the normal take-off speed for a B-25 is 80 or 90 after a run three or four times as long.

These days were dull but worrisome for the wives. Most of us were so dead tired from work that we never felt much like showing them a good time at night. This was no holiday, and they knew it. Everybody was serious. I wasn't really worried, and I don't think Ellen was. I was anxious to get in all the training I could. It was a good solid feeling to be a part of this thing, whatever it was. I wanted to know all the answers before it started. I told Ellen that when it was over we could have some time together. Maybe even have a honeymoon.

The tactical problems at Eglin were pretty fascinating. There was a lot of talk that we'd get 100-plus octane gas for the trip, but then we heard that it would be

100 octane because our 1,700 horsepower Wright engines weren't built for 100-plus octane, and, besides, the evaporation of the more combustible gas was too great. Gas consumption was now a primary issue. During the last part of the training period we made countless flights, mainly for the purpose of testing engineering findings on our best speed at the least consumption.

Finally, near the end of March, we had our big test: a quick, ear-splitting take-off, a flight to Fort Myers, Florida, then across the Gulf of Mexico at very low level to Houston, then back to Eglin. That was our final exam in Florida.

We were given little warning before leaving Eglin. We were awakened at 3 A.M. on the morning of March 24th and told that we'd take off at 11 A.M. Ellen didn't know where to go at first, but before I had to take off she and the wives of Major John Hilger and Captain Greening had decided to share a house in Myrtle Beach, South Carolina. I couldn't give her any idea how long I'd be gone, but this seemed like the best place for her. It was reasonable and quiet. It would be a good place to wait for the baby.

"I'm going to write you a letter every day you're gone," Ellen told me. "There's no hope you'll get any of them; in fact, I won't even mail them. But it will be kind of comforting to do. I'll feel closer to you." I told her I'd try to write to her a lot, but it was a long time before I did.

I took off with five other B-25's that morning of March 24th and we flew to San Antonio. We stayed there overnight and the next day we flew on to March Field, on the Coast, refueling only at Phoenix. We were still training. We were told to hedge-hop our way across the country, testing gas consumption at low levels, and we kept so low we could look up at the telegraph wires.

At our last meeting before we left, Doolittle told us that when we reached the West Coast we weren't to see or telephone anybody. But March Field is only eighty miles from home, so I thought I'd take a chance and call my mother. My mother had written us at Eglin that she had been feeling bad. I knew she must be feeling worse than bad because her last letters had been in longhand and that usually meant that she wasn't going to her office. My mother did social work with juvenile delinquents.

So I called her up that night from March Field and a nurse answered the phone. I got the nurse to put my mother on the wire, and she finally told me that she had had the first stages of a stroke. She was worried about me.

"Where are you going, Ted?" she asked me.

I told her that I was just on a routine flight. But she was suspicious. She asked where Ellen was. I told her I had left Ellen back East because I'd probably be sent back there right away. I started to tell my mother that I was sending my civilian clothes home, but I thought it might worry her.

My mother was on the phone early the next morning. She said she was worried about me. I told her that she wasn't even supposed to know where I was. It was supposed to be a secret, I tried to tell her, but that only made her more suspicious. She told me she had a bad feeling about me, and to take care of myself. I was sorry I sounded short on the phone, but I had been ordered not to call anybody. I guess I was nervous.

We had to fly up to Sacramento's McClellan Field from March Field as soon as we could. So we took off right after breakfast and flew up there, brushing the trees. All of us seemed to figure we might not be around very long, so we might as well do things we always wanted to do. It was the craziest flying I had ever done, and I had done some kid-stuff tricks, like banking a B-25 through a low, open drawbridge. We got to McClellan, feeling that we had let off a lot of pent-up steam.

Doolittle was already there. He had flown directly

from San Antonio. He went across the Rockies on instruments, instead of first going to March Field and then up the Coast line. It gave me a feeling of pride to have him in charge.

There was a meeting just after we arrived at McClellan. "I don't want any of you to raise hell tonight," Doolittle told us. "You stick close to the field. I want every first pilot to make absolutely certain that his plane is in perfect shape, and that his crew also is. They've got good mechanics here. They'll take care of anything that's wrong with your ships. I want you to instruct them to repair the smallest thing that might be wrong."

Then he told us that the radio equipment would be taken out of our planes. "You won't need it where you're going," he said.

We all sensed by now that it had something to do with the Japanese.

All twenty-four planes had new $1,500 three-bladed props put on the first day at McClellan. Then I had to stand by and watch one of the mechanics rev my engines so fast that the new blades picked up dirt which pockmarked their tips. I caught another one trying to sandpaper the imperfections away and yelled at him until he got out some oil and rubbed it on the places which he had sandpapered. I knew that salt air would make those prop tips pulpy where they had been scraped.

The way they revved our motors made us wince. All of us were so afraid that they'd hurt the ships, the way they were handling them, yet we couldn't tell them why we wanted them to be so careful. I guess we must have acted like the biggest bunch of soreheads those mechanics ever saw, but we kept beefing until Doolittle got on the long-distance phone, called Washington and had the work done the way we wanted it done.

We spent a few more days in that area, practicing full-flap take-offs at small, almost deserted fields. Then one morning we hopped over the hump to Alameda. We were on our way again; we had been training a month.

McClure had a movie camera along with a roll of colored film. He wanted to get some shots of the Bay Bridge. "What about flying under the bridge?" Davenport asked me. "The Pan American boys do it all the time in the Clippers. It would make a good shot for Mac."

Dav was at the controls. He put the nose down and we ran for the bridge. I hoped there weren't any cables hanging under the span. I was half tempted to take over and pull the Ruptured Duck up over the bridge at the last moment. But I knew what a nut McClure was about home movies, so we went underneath.

Just as we did, Mac let out a yell. He couldn't get his camera working. He wanted us to do it again, but I said to hell with it. Some time later we came to the rendezvous.

As I put the flaps down for the landing, we all let out a yell at the same time, and I guess we all got the same empty feeling in the stomach that I did.

An American aircraft carrier was underneath us. Three of our B-25's were already on its deck.

"Damn! Ain't she small," somebody said in the inter-phone.

We landed on the field and taxied over to the side where Doolittle and York were beckoning to us. I rolled back my window and looked down at them.

"Is everything okay?" Doolittle asked.

I said everything was.

"Taxi off the field and park at the edge of the *Hornet*'s wharf. They'll take care of you there," Doolittle said.

As soon as I did, the Navy boys jumped all over us. They drained out all our gas, except a few gallons. One of the boys got in, after our crew got out. An Army "donkey" hooked the Ruptured Duck's main gear and towed it down the pier. We walked down after it and then watched the claws of a big crane reach down and pick up our ship as if it weighed ten pounds. The crane swung it slowly up on the deck of the *Hornet*.

We were standing there, watching this, when Lieutenant Miller came up to me and said, "Don't tell the Navy boys anything. They don't know where you're going."

I nodded and kept looking at the *Hornet*. She was a great sight. I can't describe the feeling I got, standing there, looking up at her sides. Maybe the thing I felt was just plain patriotism. All I know is that it was a fine feeling to know that she was there and ready to help us.

It was a tremendous relief to know that our plane got on. Looking around now, I saw that Doolittle and York were sending some of the planes to a near-by hangar, instead of to the wharf. I found out, after we walked back down the pier to the field, that if I had said that anything was wrong with the ship when Doolittle asked me, we would have been rejected too. It made me suddenly weak to think how close I had come to beefing about the way the ground force at McClellan had patched up our inter-phone system.

We had lunch and talked to some of the fellows who had been turned down after all that training. Most of them were too sick with disappointment to eat. There wasn't anything to say to them that would help them. There were some other men who had been told that they would go along as spares on the mission, and they felt better. After lunch we walked back to the *Hornet*, trying to remember all the things Lieutenant Miller had told us about Navy etiquette.

Sixteen planes had been lucky. The Navy had spaced them out all over the deck of the *Hornet*, placed blocks under the wheels and now were tying the planes to the flight deck.

We all stood up on deck, not knowing quite what to do. After a while a couple of tugs nuzzled up to the *Hornet* and pulled us away from the pier. I looked around the bewildering ship and finally found my quarters. I shared a compact little room with two Ensigns, one of them a big, hearty fellow named "Nig" White.

I was a First Lieutenant then and thus outranked the Ensigns, but that didn't seem to impress them very much. They crawled into their nice bunks and pointed to a cot for me.

We began moving the next morning at nine o'clock. That first day I wandered through the ship with the rest of the Army fellows, figuring out how not to get lost. The Navy boys kidded us a lot, trying to get us to tell them where we were going. But we were mum. We just looked wise, as if we knew.

The Navy fliers were very interested in the B-25's

sprawled all over the deck. We took them all over our planes, bragging like kids about how fast and how far they could go. We were awful proud of our planes. The Navy boys returned the favor by taking us below decks and showing us their dive bombers, torpedo planes and fighters. Their wings were folded and, naturally, they were cooped up because our ships took up all the space on the flight deck. I wondered a little how the *Hornet* would protect itself.

It was late that afternoon that I realized we weren't alone. Looking around, I began to see more and more warships until finally I could see cruisers and destroyers.

The word Japan was mentioned officially for the first time the next morning. Doolittle called us together in the empty mess hall and all of us sensed that now we'd know.

He cleared his throat and said, "For the benefit of those of you who don't already know, or who have been guessing, we are going straight to Japan. We're going to bomb Tokyo, Yokohama, Osaka, Kobe and Nagoya. The Navy is going to take us in as close as is advisable, and, of course, we're going to take off from the deck."

I can't tell you how much of a relief it was to hear these words. It took away the weeks of confused thinking and ended a period of hush that was griping all of us. I could stand up and yell Japan at the top of my lungs now. I was no longer shooting in the dark. Here was a job, definite and tangible. My thoughts went to my plane—the condition it was in—the gas it would burn—the distance we'd travel. . . .

Doolittle was talking. "It's going to be a pretty tight squeeze," he said. "But it's all been worked out the best possible way. The Chinese government will co-operate with us. We've made complete arrangements to land at small Chinese fields not far inland—after we've done our bombing. We'll tank up at the small field—the gas is there, waiting for us—and then we'll fly on to Chungking. Now, we're going to be on this carrier a long time, but there will be plenty of work for you to do before we take off."

Again he gave us a chance to back out, in favor of one of the spare men brought along. But, of course, nobody did.

When the meeting broke up, all of us drifted instinctively to our planes. Some of the boys walked along the flight deck, measuring off the alarmingly short distance between the island and the bow. You see, we didn't have to be told that we'd be able to use only about half the deck. We knew there wouldn't be any place to put the sixteen parked planes, except to squeeze them in together on the stern. Even then we figured that they'd take up nearly half the deck. So the boys who were pacing off the probable distance we'd have for a take-off were measuring from the middle of the island to the bow. And scratching their heads at the end of their pacing.

I handed out pads of paper among the crew of the Ruptured Duck and told McClure, Clever, Davenport and Thatcher to jot down everything that came to their minds that would get the ship in better condition. I didn't have to tell them how important this was to all of us. We tinkered around the plane most of the day. After dark McClure and I went up to the bridge to test our navigation. The Navy was ready to do anything we asked. There had been a couple of officers at the meeting that morning, and the word was filtering through the ship. When I got to my quarters this second night out, the two Ensigns shook hands with me and insisted that I sleep thereafter in the better of their two soft bunks.

We began to realize just how incredibly well planned the mission was the following day. At the meeting, Doolittle introduced us to two Naval officers—Lieutenant Commander Stephen Jurika and Commander Apollo Soucek, Executive Officers of the *Hornet*. Jurika had been Naval Attaché at our Embassy at Tokyo and now he gave us the first of a series of lectures. It seemed curious at first, but soon I could see how much we needed it. He spoke on the history of Japan and China. He went into detail about the political setups of the countries, told us of the differences between the military and peasant classes of Japan, the psychological differences between Chinese and Japanese, described the various modes of dress and uniforms we might encounter and physiological differences.

More and more we realized the seriousness of the mission. When Jurika finished, Doolittle grinned reassuringly at us and said, "Well, if we all get to Chungking, I'll throw the biggest Goddamn party you ever saw."

We worked hard on the *Hornet*, day and night. There was always something to do or test around the plane. At night, when our bunch would work inside the ship, we'd put up cardboard over the windows of the Ruptured Duck in deference to the blackout on the ship. In addition, there was a lot of studying. Doolittle placed Davey Jones in charge of our map room. Davey put us to work early on the job of memorizing cities and geographical landmarks along the course we planned to use on the raid. He also had dozens of aerial photographs of the five Japanese cities marked out to be bombed, and told us to get an indelible picture of them in our minds.

All of us got a scare, the third day out, that we'd miss the raid. The Navy boys came out with buckets of white paint and drew a line along the port side, two or three yards in from the edge. We heard that Doolittle had decided to send one of the planes back to the mainland with a message. The message couldn't be sent any other way because the *Hornet* was observing radio silence. I tried to keep out of Doolittle's sight as much as possible, and so did the others. The line, of course, was to be the guide of the plane ordered to take off. It was easy to figure out that the left wheel of the unlucky B-25 selected would have to keep on that line. In order to clear the island with the tip of the right wing, the fuselage of the plane had to be quite far over to the left, and the left wing would extend out over the edge of the ship.

Our fears subsided after the line was drawn. A Navy blimp came over to us, hovered over the deck, dropped us some stuff, and presumably took back the necessary messages that had to be transmitted to the mainland. It was a relief to know that I hadn't gone through all that training just to become a messenger boy.

Doolittle gave us the right to choose the city we

wanted to bomb. When it came my turn to speak I said our bunch wanted to take a look at Tokyo. My study of the four Chinese fields where we could land and refuel also convinced me that our best bet would be the field at Choo Chow Lishui, about 100 miles inland.

Our bombing problem was complicated. We were told we would drop three 500-pound bombs where they would do the most military damage, yet drop them in the shortest space of time and on as much of a straight line as possible. This was to give us the least possible amount of anti-aircraft fire. We went over heavily detailed maps of the city of Tokyo with Jurika.

"I know that town like a book," he'd say, and give us the location of this or that factory or plant. Finally, we selected three targets on a reasonably straight line and close together, and we began the long job of memorizing their characteristics. We were going to be able to take a few maps along with us, but no pictures, and there were to be no lines or erasures of ours showing on the maps, for fear that if they were captured it might in some way lead the Japs back to the Navy.

Doolittle also told us that we would carry another bomb, a 500-pound incendiary, something like the old Russian Molotov Breadbasket. This would have to be dropped also from a low altitude. The inflammable section should be as near as possible to the other targets, so that we could let the incendiary go and then dive down out of the range of anti-aircraft fire.

"If you can start seven good fires in Tokyo, they'll never put them out," Jurika promised us. "I know that Tokyo fire department very well. Seven big scattered fires would be too much for it to cope with. I wouldn't worry too much about setting fires in flimsy-looking sections of Tokyo," he said. "The Japanese have done an amazing job of spreading out some of their industries, instead of concentrating them in large buildings. There's probably a small machine shop under half of these fragile-looking roofs."

At the next meeting, in answer to a question, Doolittle said that there would be no bombing of the palace. He said it wasn't worth a plane factory or a steel smelter or a tank farm. It was at the same meeting that we were instructed on the shapes, sizes, silhouettes and abilities of every known type of Japanese plane. We were told that the Japs have a bomber similar to the B-25, and that there would be some slight chance that we would be mistaken for Japanese bombers when we came over. But the main expectation was that they'd throw everything they could get in the air against us.

At Eglin our bombing plans were all based on night flights. That presented the problem of barrage balloons, and I envisioned running into their cables in the dark.

We left our ships, guns, instruments, charts, maps, pictures and lectures only to eat and sleep. The Navy fattened us up like condemned men. We even had chicken. Most of us gained weight and very few of us were seasick. There was too much to think about. Back on land we would have considered our ships in the greatest shape of their lives, but with so much now depending on little things, we found a hundred and one things to straighten out. I told Thatcher that every minute counted and to stop calling me "Sir" because it was a waste of time.

"All right, sir, I won't," he said seriously.

We swung readily into the Navy routine. Twice a day over the loudspeakers would come the nasal command, "General quarters! Man your battle stations!" It usually came just before dawn and at dusk. Wherever we were and whatever we were doing, we'd scramble up the ladders and passageways and take our posts.

We were more than spectators at these drills. Doolittle had told us in one of the meetings that if we were attacked from the air we would have to get our planes off the deck in a hurry, and, with that in mind, we always knew just where we were and the direction and distance of the closest friendly land. If we were attacked by a surface vessel, particularly at long range, we were to leave the planes where they were and depend on the *Hornet's* guns and the heavier guns of the accompanying warships.

The only battle-stations' cry that I ignored came when we were about one week out. The late call to stations was sounded just as a mess boy was bringing two whole hot blueberry pies to Lieutenant Denver Truelove (of Lula, Georgia) and me, at the long table where our bunch ate. Everybody else at the table made a beeline for the flight deck. I took one look at the pies that were coming in and so did Truelove. We sat there and finished off both pies, though it was a kind of funny feeling, what with the Navy bolting the bulkheads and locking us in. The pie was perfect.

Early in April, north of Hawaii, our force was joined by other destroyers and cruisers. We were not a sizable task force.

We proceeded slowly west. The weather turned very bad just after the rendezvous. One of our own ships became partially crippled and could not make better than six knots. The Navy worked on it for three days and added keenly to our ever-increasing respect for the Navy. Once, while in motion, a heavy wave swept over one of our ships and washed a man overboard. Our loudspeaker system immediately and dispassionately bawled at the ship, "You've lost a man! Man overboard!"

"Okay, *Hornet*," the voice of the ship answered, and a destroyer fished him out well behind us as we kept going.

The weather was so rough at this time that once, in checking over the instrument board of the Ruptured Duck, I noticed that the rise and dip of the *Hornet* would affect our altimeter as much as 200 feet.

There was now no radio communication among the ships of the force. In fact, we weren't permitted to use our personal radio receiving sets or electric razors.

The days were crowded with lectures, tinkering and practice for the gunners. The *Hornet* let out kites behind the ship to give our men practice shooting at them. The *Hornet* had no way of using its own planes, which may or may not have accounted for the frequent firing practice of its guns. Its "Chicago pianos," those multi-barreled pom poms, gave out with the darnedest musical scale you ever heard—a grim broken chord of three or four sharp notes. *Hornet* gunners would pour a perfect curtain of fire into the sky. Other ships frequently tried their guns, too, to add to the growing tension. Cruisers catapulted scout planes for long trips to all sides of our force, while we worked. Working on the plane one day with all this going on, I suddenly realized how much it was all costing. It made me want to carry out my end.

Much worse than the scare about being sent back with a message, was the sick feeling all of us got when word spread through the ship that Tokyo had been bombed by four-motored American planes. Getting there first had never mattered much until then. We were a sourly disgruntled bunch until Doolittle told us it wasn't true. That was great news and made us that much keener. The rumor was a garbled report of the Royce raid on the Philippines.

I guess I was a nut about the Ruptured Duck, for the boys played a trick on me one day about this time, and it nearly turned me gray. One of them ran up to me, below decks, and told me that the "donkey" which the Navy had parked on the flight deck had broken loose and crashed into my plane, knocking in my ship's side. I ran like a crazy man until I got to the Ruptured Duck, and I was so glad that it was a gag that I couldn't get too sore at the fellows who pulled it. At that, it helped relieve the mounting pressure on all of us.

Our task force was in the command of Admiral Halsey, aboard the *Hornet*. We got a good look at him on the 15th. He came out to pose for Navy newsreel men, along with Doolittle and a row of the bombs we were going to use. All of us crowded around to watch the show.

It was very interesting. Naval officers who had been decorated by the Japanese during the peace years had turned in their medals after Pearl Harbor. Someone, I don't know who, thought it would be a good idea to tie the medals to the bombs we were going to drop. So they were brought along on the *Hornet*.

Halsey tied one on to one of the fat 500-pounders, for the benefit of the newsreels, and then he turned that good, tough face to us and said, "Boys, return these medals with interest. Good hunting."

At the meeting that day, Doolittle read us some messages of good will from Admiral King, General Marshall and General Arnold. It was a strange feeling to realize that men far behind us in Washington were plotting for us and rooting for us and that thousands of miles ahead of us men were prepared to help us. The enormity of the plan was too stunning to contemplate.

The messages were fine. They contained a little soft stuff that we all appreciated. One of them said that our deed would live forever—that the people would be deeply grateful to us.

Gasoline was my main worry toward the end. I would lie in my bunk with an ear-splitting card game going on in the same room until the small hours of the

morning, and the thought of getting enough gas in my
ship would never leave my mind. Maybe I thought too
much about gas down in our room. Before I admitted
defeat, the Navy poker players had pared the $70 I
brought aboard to $14. You never saw such poker
players!

This was to be our gas load: our wing tanks carried
500 gallons, and to that would be added the emergency
tank, the bullet-proof tank in the opening where the
bottom gun turret had been, another metal tank that
fitted into the top of the bomb bay and ten five-gallon
cans. The Ruptured Duck burned about twice as much
at full throttle as at cruising speed. I began wondering
how much use I'd have to make of full throttle.

So I went to Doolittle one day toward the end and
told him that I had been figuring our probable gas consumption and asked him if I could carry twenty-five
five-gallon cans in the plane instead of the ten he had
allotted us. I told him I realized that the extra gas would
weigh six pounds a gallon but that I was sure my ship
could take it.

"No," he said. "Your tail might get sluggish with
that extra four hundred and fifty pounds in there. It
might start whipping around, and there's not going to
be a lot of room to do that. The first important thing
you've got to do is get off this deck. If you can't do that,

well, we will have wasted a helluva lot of time and money."

I told him I thought the extra weight would make me steadier and easier to get off, but he couldn't see it my way. I went away, wondering what made me keep thinking the Navy would not be able to get us as close to Japan as promised.

We had our orders about discarding the five-gallon cans. "I don't want you to throw them out as they're used," Doolittle told us in a meeting when that question came up. "If you do, it will leave a perfect trail for the Japanese to follow back to the carrier. Use up the stuff in the cans first, of course, but save them and dump them all together. The Navy has been great to us. Let's show our appreciation in whatever way we can.

"Another thing: If any of you men are foolish enough to carry anything that might lead the enemy back to the Navy, in case you're forced down and captured, get rid of it now."

That was the day I gave back the ash tray one of the Navy boys had made for me, with the word *Hornet* on it. Incidentally, that was the only spelling out of the name I saw on the entire ship, except on the dried-up hornet's nest that hung in the wardroom.

The time was getting near. We were going to take

off during the evening of Sunday, April 19th, come in over our cities in the dark and fly the rest of the way during the remainder of the night, landing after dawn in China. Our carrier would turn back and escape during the night. And, with the time drawing near, Doolittle was as restless for action as any of us. He inspected all of our planes. When he came to our ship he gave me permission to take out the seat-adjustment mechanism, to enable us to push our seats back farther than they ordinarily went. He thought it would facilitate our movement in the plane. He told us for the hundredth time that our navigation would have to be perfect.

He climbed up in our ship and immediately noticed that somebody had hooked an inter-phone headset near our compass. He told us to keep headsets and all other magnetic properties as far away from the compass as possible. To prove his point he held one of our thermos bottles over the compass, and its needle swerved thirty degrees. He told us not to get any of our automatics close to the compass.

We were one-man arsenals. Each of us was given at least one .45, a clip of ammunition, a hunting knife, flashlight, emergency rations, morphine, sterilized bandages, holsters and straps to hold these things to us, a canteen, compass and life jacket. We were walking magnets, and the thought of that sent us back to our maps again. We had them down pretty fine, but it was a little disturbing to have the Navy boys tell us that best available maps of the China coast line failed to show correctly its numerous coves, irregularities and the islands that skirt it.

Lieutenant Don Smith, of Belle Fourche, South Dakota had additional headaches. Smitty's right engine cracked a high blower on the 16th while he was testing it. The Navy was ready for that, among many other things. Navy carpenters built a platform up to the engine, mechanics took the big power plant off in a hurry, sent it down to the machine shops, fixed it and put it back on Smitty's wing.

Near the end, Doolittle called us together, gave us one last chance to back out, and nobody did. Captain York then asked whether any of the first pilots wanted changes in their crews. One did; he released his co-pilot and selected another from the ten substitutes we carried on board.

On April 17th, which turned out to be our last full day on the *Hornet*, our rear gun turret went bad.

We worked like fools on the turret, appreciating more than ever how much we'd have to depend on it. Japanese planes would certainly attack us, we felt, and our rear guns were our main protection.

As we worked, the tension mounted on the ship. The *Hornet* was pulling away from the force, accompanied by spray-spouting cruisers and knifing destroyers. The carrier shuddered with new power and we plunged deeper and deeper into Japanese controlled waters. We were a little more than 1,000 miles off Japan now. We were coming into the homestretch, and everybody knew it. We worked on and cursed the turret.

There were so many things to think about, without the worry of the turret. My head was full of lectures, maps, charts, photographs of our targets, the worry over gas and a thousand and one other details. Those barrage balloons, for instance. My mind formed pictures of hitting the cables of one of them, in the night, and having our wings sheared off, or our props hopelessly fouled.

I tried to get that off my mind by making myself think about something else. Something trivial it was, too. Ever since the Navy had clipped my bankroll to $14 I had been wondering how I'd get hold of enough to buy something for Ellen and my mother, if all went well and I got to Chungking. So that last day, when I took time out for a quick dinner, I decided that I'd recoup my poker losses by becoming a cigarette-runner. I had heard that cigarettes sold for $7.50 a carton in

Chungking and that there is never enough to meet the demand. They were a nickel a pack on the *Hornet*, so I stocked up. When I went back to the plane, to work on the turret, I packed eight cartons and two boxes of chocolate bars in the rear of the plane.

I was tuckered out and discouraged about the turret that night of the 17th by the time I got to my bunk. "Nig" White was just shuffling the cards and some of the Navy boys were drifting in, readying for another night of it. They watched me come in and asked me if I wanted to take a hand. I told them no, thanks, and then one of them did a real decent thing. He said, "Listen, you fellows, there's going to be no card playing in here tonight. Lawson's got to get some sleep for a change. He might need it."

I did.

I slept from about ten o'clock until battle stations the next dawn—which regrettably and unexpectedly turned out to be the day of the raid. That was April 18th.

After battle stations early that morning I went back to the room to wait for breakfast. I thought it would be a good idea to see just how much equipment I could get in my B-4 bag. All of us had B-4's. It's a valise, canvaslike, which is packed in a flat, spread-out fashion, then folded into handier carrying shape. It can be hung up, unfolded, to keep your stuff pressed.

I tried putting in my raincoat, shaving kit, shoes, shirts, shorts, handkerchiefs, blouse, trousers, and a few other things. It was about 7:30 A.M., bitterly cold and rough.

That's when it happened. First there was a muffled, vibrating roar, followed immediately by the husky cry of battle stations. "Nig" jumped for the door and I went right after him. We were three decks down. Scrambling after "Nig" as fast as I could, I found other Army boys racing for the top. We flung questions at one another, but got no answers. And twice before I could get up on top, the *Hornet* vibrated and echoed with the sound of heavy gun-fire near by.

I got out on the flight deck and ran around a B-25 just in time to see the cruiser off to our left let go another broadside of flame in the direction away from us. And presently, down near the horizon, a low-slung ship began to give off an ugly plume of black smoke. Dive bombers were wheeling over it.

I must have asked two dozen questions in one minute. One of the Navy boys, hurrying past, said it was a Japanese patrol boat and that our gunnery had accounted for it within three minutes after engaging.

"God damn! Let's go!" somebody yelled at me above the bellow of the cruiser's guns, the crashing sea, the sound of the wind and the cries of excited, jubilant men. I turned and saw it was "Nig." He was racing back over the route we had covered just a few minutes before.

I was on his heels, saying nothing. This was it, and before we wanted it. We'd have to take off now. Not Sunday evening. Now, Saturday morning. We were forced to assume that the Japanese ship had had time to flash the warning about us. All hope of surprising the Japanese had now fled, I thought. Surprise was our main safety factor, Doolittle had often drummed into our heads. We had no way of knowing that no warning was sent. Apparently the ship either did not see the B-25's spread all over the deck of the *Hornet*, or just couldn't believe that it was possible, or maybe the Navy sank it too soon.

The *Hornet* leaped forward, boring a hole in the head wind. I could feel its turbines take up a faster beat and felt that it was straining forward as fast as it could, to get us a minute closer—a gallon nearer.

I felt this, too: that our Navy had done all that it could—and it had done it in a way that made a fellow proud of belonging to the same country. I thought of Halsey with that tough jaw jutting out, standing high up in the island of the *Hornet*, and I wondered, as I began stuffing something in my bag, how long it would take the long-range Japanese bombers to come out after our carrier.

I don't really remember what I stuffed in my bag. Whatever it was it was handy to reach. Now I was thinking about our gas, and the junking of so many of our long-discussed plans. We had based so much of our hope of getting to China on the presumption that the Navy could run us up to within about 400 miles of the Japanese coast. Even then it was going to be a tight fit.

Now we were going to take off about 800 miles off the coast. It took some figuring—quick figuring. And the sums I arrived at, in my buzzing head, gave me a sudden emptiness in the stomach. I thought of the preparations the Japanese must be making for us, and I thought of that turret that just wouldn't work. But most of all I thought of our gas.

"Army pilots, man your planes! Army pilots, man your planes!" the loud speakers brayed. But I already knew the time had come. "Nig" was a great help. He helped me round up my gun, compass, medical stuff and the whisky. Lieutenant Thomas R. White, the mission's flight surgeon—and, inevitably, "Doc" to everybody—had brought along eighty quarts of GI bourbon—a quart for each man who was going on the raid. On the ship, Doc traded it in for pints of Navy medicinal rye. Easier to carry, if we had to bail out.

"Nig" and I started up top with our arms filled. "Nig" was pretty talkative. I guess he could see I was nervous. He asked me if I thought it would be a good idea to relax a moment and take a drink out of one of the pints. I don't even remember answering him.

I went right to my plane. The crew was there. I shoved the whisky and some of the other stuff in Mc-Clure's navigating compartment, just behind and a step lower than the pilot's compartment.

The flight deck of the *Hornet* was alive with activity, while the big voice of the looming island barked commands. The man I thought was responsible for our bad turret hurried by and I stopped him long enough to tell him what I thought of him. And was sorry, as soon as I did. Nothing was important now except getting off that wet, rolling deck.

Lieutenant Jack "Shorty" Manch, a Virginian who must be the tallest fellow in the Air Force, ran up to our plane, carrying a fruit-cake tin.

"Hey, Clever," he said to our bombardier, "will you-all do a fellow a big favor and carry my phonograph records under your seat? I'll take my record-player along in my plane and we'll meet in

Chungking and have us some razz-ma-tazz," and Shorty practically trucked on away from us through the turmoil. Clever shrugged and put the can of hot records under his seat.

The Navy was now taking charge, and doing it with an efficiency which made our popped eyes pop some more. Blocks were whipped out from under wheels. The whirring little "donkey"—the same one that was supposed to have broken loose and smashed my plane—was pushing and pulling the B-25's into position.

In about half an hour the Navy had us criss-crossed along the back end of the flight deck, two abreast, the big double-rudder tail assemblies of the sixteen planes sticking out of the edges of the rear of the ship at an angle. From the air, the *Hornet*, with its slim, clean foredeck, and its neatly cluttered rear deck, must have looked like an arrow with pin-feathers abounding along the surface of the water.

It was good enough flying weather, but the sea was tremendous. The *Hornet* bit into the rough-house waves, dipping and rising until the flat deck was a crazy see-saw. Some of the waves actually were breaking over the deck. The deck seemed to grow smaller by the minute, and I had a brief fear of being hit by a wave on the take-off and of crashing at the end of the deck and falling off into the path of the careening carrier.

The *Hornet*'s speed rose until it was making its top speed, that hectic, hurried perfect morning of April 18th. The bombs now came up from below and rolled along the deck on their low-slung lorries to our planes. It was our first look at the 500-pound incendiary; but we didn't waste much time on it except to see that it was placed in the bomb bay so that it could be released fourth and last.

The Navy had fueled our planes previously, but now they topped the tanks. That was to take care of any evaporation that might have set in. When the gauges read full, groups of the Navy boys rocked our planes in the hope of breaking whatever bubbles had formed in the big wing tanks, for that might mean that we could take a few more quarts. The *Hornet*'s control tower was now beginning to display large square cards, giving us compass readings, and the wind, which was of gale proportions.

I saw our take-off instructor, Lieutenant Miller, trot up to Doolittle's plane and climb in the bottom opening. For a time I thought that he was going along, but after a bit he came out and began visiting each of the other B-25's. We were in the Ruptured Duck now, all of us, and when Miller came up to the pilot's compartment he must have stood there a half minute with his hand stuck out at me before I came back to life and shook hands with him. I had so much on my mind. Miller wished all of us good luck, and he said, "I wish to hell I could go with you."

It was something of a relief when five additional five-gallon tins of gas were handed in to us. We lined them up in the fuselage beside the ten cans Doolittle had already allotted us. It was a sobering thought to realize that we were going to have to fly at least 400 miles farther than we had planned. But my concern over that, as I sat there in the plane waiting to taxi and edge up to the starting line, was erased by a sudden relief that now we wouldn't have to worry about running into barrage balloons at night. This, of course, was going to be a daylight raid. It was only a few minutes after eight in the morning.

Commander Jurika and "Nig" also came up to say good-bye and to shake hands. When they had gone I suddenly remembered that none of my crew had had breakfast and that all of us had lost sight of the fact that we could have taken coffee and water and sandwiches along. I was tempted to send Clever below to get some food, but I was afraid that there would not be time. Besides, Doolittle's ship was being pulled up to the starting line and his and other props were beginning to turn. The *Hornet's* deck wasn't a safe place. I found out later that one of the Navy boys had an arm clipped off by a propellor blade that morning.

Doolittle warmed and idled his engines, and now we got a vivid demonstration of one of our classroom lectures on how to get a 25,000-pound bomber off half the deck of a carrier.

A Navy man stood at the bow of the ship, and off to the left, with a checkered flag in his hand. He gave Doolittle, who was at the controls, the signal to begin racing his engines again. He did it by swinging the flag in a circle and making it go faster and faster. Doolittle gave his engines more and more throttle until I was afraid that he'd burn them up. A wave crashed heavily at the bow and sprayed the deck.

Then I saw that the man with the flag was waiting, timing the dipping of the ship so that Doolittle's plane would get the benefit of a rising deck for its take-off. Then the man gave a new signal. Navy boys pulled the blocks from under Doolittle's wheels. Another signal and Doolittle released his brakes and the bomber moved forward.

With full flaps, motors at full throttle and his left wing far out over the port side of the *Hornet,* Doolittle's plane waddled and then lunged slowly into the teeth of the gale that swept down the deck. His left wheel stuck on the white line as if it were a track. His right wing, which had barely cleared the wall of the island as he taxied and was guided up to the starting line, extended nearly to the edge of the starboard side.

We watched him like hawks, wondering what the wind would do to him, and whether we could get off in that little run toward the bow. If he couldn't, we couldn't.

Doolittle picked up more speed and held to his line, and, just as the *Hornet* lifted itself up on the top of a wave and cut through it at full speed, Doolittle's plane took off. He had yards to spare. He hung his ship almost straight up on its props, until we could see the whole top of his B-25. Then he leveled off and I watched him come around in a tight circle and shoot low over our heads—straight down the line painted on the deck.

The *Hornet* was giving him his bearings. Admiral Halsey had headed it for the heart of Tokyo.

The engines of three other ships were warming up, and the thump and hiss of the turbulent sea made additional noise. But loud and clear above those sounds I could hear the hoarse cheers of every Navy man on the ship. They made the *Hornet* fairly shudder with their yells—and I've never heard anything like it, before or since.

Travis Hoover went off second and nearly crashed. Brick Holstrom was third; Bob Gray, fourth; Davey Jones, fifth; Dean Hallmark, sixth, and I was seventh.

I was on the line now, my eyes glued on the man with the flag. He gave me the signal to put my flaps down. I reached down and drew the flap lever back and down. I checked the electrical instrument that indicates whether the flaps are working. They were. I could feel the plane quaking with the strain of having the flat surface of the flaps thrust against the gale and the blast from the props. I got a sudden fear that they might blow off and cripple us, so I pulled up the flaps again, and I guess the Navy man understood. He let it go and began giving me the signal to rev my engines.

I liked the way they sounded long before he did. There had been a moment, earlier, when I had an agonizing fear that something was wrong with the left engine. It wouldn't start, at first. But I had gotten it going, good. Now, after fifteen seconds of watching the man with the flag spinning his arm faster and faster, I began to worry again. He must know his stuff, I tried to tell myself, but when, for God's sake, would he let me go?

I thought of all the things that could go wrong at this last minute. Our instructions along these lines were simple and to the point. If a motor quit or caught fire, if a tire went flat, if the right wing badly scraped the island, if the left wheel went over the edge, we were to get out as quickly as we could and help the Navy shove our $150,000 plane overboard. It must not, under any circumstances, be permitted to block traffic. There would be no other way to clear the forward deck for the other planes to take off.

After thirty blood-sweating seconds the Navy man was satisfied with the sound of my engines. Our wheel blocks were jerked out, and when I released the brakes we quivered forward, the wind grabbing at the wings. We rambled dangerously close to the edge, but I braked in time, got the left wheel back on the white line and picked up speed. The *Hornet's* deck bucked wildly. A sheet of spray rushed back at us.

I never felt the take-off. One moment the end of the *Hornet's* flight deck was rushing at us alarmingly fast; the next split-second I glanced down hurriedly at what had been a white line, and it was water. There was no drop nor any surge into the air. I just went off at deck level and pulled out in front of the great ship that had done its best to plant us in Japan's front yard.

I banked now, gaining a little altitude, and instinctively reached down to pull up the flaps. With a start I realized that they were not down. I had taken off without using them.

I swung around as Doolittle and the others before me had done, came over the nine remaining planes on the deck, got the bearing and went on—hoping the others would get off and that the *Hornet*—God rest her—would get away in time.

There was no rendezvous planned, except at the end of the mission. Those who took off early could not hover over the ship until a formation was formed because that would have burned too much gas in the first planes. This was to be a single file, hit-and-run raid—each plane for itself. And at levels which still are hard to believe.

Once on our way, we immediately started topping the wing tanks with the auxiliary gas. We began with the big emergency tank. I knew all there was to know about the appetite of our Wrights, but it was still depressing to figure that they had burned the equivalent of eight of our five-gallon tins during the warming up and take-off. Forty precious gallons gone before we were on our way!

About 2,200 miles of non-stop flying, I hoped, lay ahead of us. I tried now to visualize the end of the trip, the airport at Choo Chow Lishui. I thought again of the tremendous planning behind the whole raid when I recalled that I must not miss the signals at Choo Chow Lishui or the other Chinese fields I might be tempted to choose. All of them were close to Japanese-occupied territory. There was always the chance that even while we were en route the Japanese might seize these fields. If that happened, the Chinese were to signal "Don't land" by a simple but effective system.

But there were more pressing things to think about now as I kept the clean nose of the Ruptured Duck about twenty feet above the water and settled into the gas-saving groove. If all went well on the way in, I would hit Tokyo about a half hour after Doolittle. I figured that if by some improbable miracle the first few planes got in unmolested every Japanese fighting plane and anti-aircraft gun would be ready for me, and for the others behind me.

That made me think about the turret. I pushed the button on the inter-phone and told Thatcher to give it one more test. He did and said it was still on the blink. Then I switched on the emergency juice, but that wouldn't work either. I hadn't built up enough power as yet. Our two 50-calibre rear guns were pointing straight back between the twin rudders and would be unable to budge one way or the other in case of attack. I spoke to Thatcher again and said that, at least, we'd test the guns. So I raised the nose of the plane and, when the tail slanted down at the right angle, Thatcher fired a short burst into the water behind us.

"Damn, boy, this is serious," Davenport, the co-pilot, said into the phone.

We plowed along at a piddling speed for a B-25. The controls were very sloppy at that speed. Nobody wanted to say anything. We were busy, or thinking. The flying weather was good—disgustingly good.

Suddenly a dazzling, twisting object rushed past our left wing. It was startling until I realized it was a five-gallon can discarded by one of the planes in front of me. I could see two planes, and Thatcher said he could see two behind us. The can would have downed us if it had hit a prop. What a climax that would have been!

An hour and a half after we took off we came into view of a large Japanese merchantman. It was about three miles off to our left as we spun along just over the waves.

"Let's drop one on it," Davenport said into the phone.

"Let's do," somebody else said. I let them talk. I had better use for the bombs.

"Okay," McClure said, "but I bet that guy is radio-ing plenty to Tokyo about us." It was the only ship we saw on the way in, but no one doubted by now that the whole coast of Japan knew that we were en route.

Our emergency tank was used up by now and we were well into our other stores. We drummed along, expecting to see planes every minute, but saw none. I tried the turret again, and it worked. I had enough power. It had to be used clumsily in that the emergency power had to be turned on in the pilot's compartment. I couldn't see Thatcher in the back of the plane, so it had to be done over the phone. The emergency power would last such a short time that the turret would have to be used sparingly. Only during actual attack could I afford to turn it on.

We kept going in and, after two or three hours, it got tiring. I was keyed up enough, but at our low level and sluggish speed it was a job to fly the ship. I called Clever on the phone, out in the snout of the bombardier's section, and asked him to turn on our automatic pilot. He did, but when I took my hands off the controls the Ruptured Duck slipped off dangerously to the left. The automatic pilot wasn't working.

So Davenport and I took turns at the controls, and I happened to have them in my hands, at 2 P.M., our time, when we sighted the coast of Japan.

It lay very low in the water in a slight haze that made it blend lacily into the horizon. I had an ingrained, picture-postcard concept of Japan. I expected to spot some snow-topped mountain or volcano first. But here was land that barely rose above the surface of the water and, at our twenty feet of height, was hardly distinguishable. I headed straight for the beach.

Many small boats were anchored off the beach and, as we came in closer, I was surprised to see that they were motor boats and nice-looking fishing launches instead of the junks I expected. I had to keep low to avoid spotters as much as possible and to keep out of range of any detecting device which the Japanese might have. So I braced myself as we came close to the masts of the little boats off shore, waiting for a burst of machine-gun fire.

We thundered up to and just over them. Instead of bullets, I got a fleeting, frozen-action look at a dozen or so men and women on the little boats. They were waving at us. You see, the emblems on our plane were the old style: blue circle with white star and a red ball in the middle of the white star. Maybe that's what confused them. I'm sure we weren't being hailed as liberators.

White beaches blended quickly into soft, rolling green fields. It was the first land I had seen in nearly three weeks. It looked very pretty. Everything seemed as well kept as a big rock garden. The little farms were fitted in with almost mathematical precision. The fresh spring grass was brilliantly green. There were fruit trees in bloom, and farmers working in their fields waved to us as we pounded just over their heads. A red lacquered temple loomed before us, its coloring exceedingly sharp. I put the nose of the ship up a little, cleared the temple, and got down lower again.

It was all so interesting that I believe none of us thought much about our danger. What brought that to us, a few minutes after we came over the land, was the sudden sight and disappearance of a large flat building which literally erupted children as we came up to it. A lot of them waved to us. I caught a fleeting glimpse of a playground—and then a sharp, quick look at a tall flagpole from which fluttered the Japanese flag.

It was like getting hit in the chest very hard. This was for keeps. I listened with new interest to the voice of the engines. A lot of the unreal beauty left the land below us. We just could not have a forced landing now.

I clicked on the inter-phone and said, "Keep your eyes open, Thatcher."

"I'm looking," Thatcher said.

I found a valley leading more or less toward Tokyo and went down it lower than the hills on either side. But McClure checked our course and found that it was leading us off, so I lifted the nose over a hill and found another valley that compensated and straightened us out again. McClure held a stop watch on the valleys that went off on tangents. He'd let me go fifteen seconds down one, then I'd hop the ridge and find one that brought us back on our imaginary beam. We kept very low.

Davenport, Clever and I saw the Zeros simultaneously. There were six of them, flying in two tight V's. They were at about 1,500 feet, coming straight at us. Our eyes followed them as they came closer and closer. They looked like one of our American racing planes, with their big air-cooled engine and stubby wings. I kept just over the tops of a forest of evergreens.

The first echelon of Zeros swept up our transparent nose and disappeared in the metal top that shut off our view. The second V of Japanese planes was now doing likewise, but just before I lost sight of them overhead the Zero on the left end peeled off and started to dive for us.

I clicked the inter-phone just as Thatcher did. "I saw him," he said.

I was relieved, until I thought again about the turret. I told Thatcher to tell me when he wanted the power on.

Five or six interminable seconds dragged by. Then I asked Thatcher if he wanted the turret on now.

"No, wait awhile," he said.

My mind was making pictures of that Zero diving on our tail with cannon and machine-gun fire. I called Thatcher again. There was no answer. I thought that something might have gone wrong with the interphone and that Thatcher even now might be yelling into a dead phone that he needed the turret. I was just about to take a chance and switch it on when Thatcher came back on the phone again.

"I don't know what the hell happened to him," he said. "I can't see him now. I think he must have gone back in the formation."

We skimmed along. We went over the rooftops of a few small villages, and I began to worry. Twenty minutes was what it was supposed to take to reach Tokyo from the point where we came in. Now we had been over land for nearly thirty minutes, and no sign of the city. I saw one fairly large town off to the left, however, and I said to myself that if worse came to worst and we couldn't find Tokyo, I'd come back there and do at least some damage.

But just then we came up over a hill, dusting the top of another temple, and there before us, as smooth as glass, lay Tokyo Bay.

It was brilliant in the mid-day sun and looked as limitless as an ocean. I came down to within about fifteen feet, while McClure checked our course. I kept the same slow speed, gas-saving but nerve-racking when I thought occasionally of the 400 mph plus diving speed of the Zeros.

We were about two minutes out over the bay when all of us seemed to look to the right at the same time and there sat the biggest, fattest-looking aircraft carrier we had ever seen. It was a couple of miles away, anchored, and there did not seem to be a man in sight. It was an awful temptation not to change course and drop one on it. But we had been so drilled in what to do with our four bombs, and Tokyo was now so close, that I decided to go on.

There were no enemy planes in sight. Ahead, I could see what must have been Davey Jones climbing fast and hard and running into innocent-looking black clouds that appeared around his plane.

It took about five minutes to get across our arm of the bay, and, while still over the water, I could see the barrage balloons strung between Tokyo and Yokohama, across the river from Tokyo.

There were no beaches where we came in. Every inch of shoreline was taken up with wharves. I could see some dredging operations filling in more shoreline, just as we were told we would see. We came in over some of the most beautiful yachts I've ever seen, then

over the heavier ships at the wharves and low over the
first of the rooftops. I gave the ship a little more throttle
for we seemed to be creeping along.

In days and nights of dreaming about Tokyo and
thinking of the eight million who live there, I got the
impression that it would be crammed together, concentrated, like San Francisco. Instead it spreads all over
creation, like Los Angeles. There is an aggressively
modern sameness to much of it and now, as we came in
very low over it, I had a bad feeling that we wouldn't
find our targets. I had to stay low and thus could see
only a short distance ahead and to the sides. I couldn't
go up to take a good look without drawing anti-aircraft
fire, which I figured would be very accurate by now because the planes that had come in ahead of me all had
bombed from 1,500 feet. The buildings grew taller. I
couldn't see people.

I was almost on the first of our objectives before I
saw it. I gave the engines full throttle as Davenport ad-
justed the prop pitch to get a better grip on the air. We
climbed as quickly as possible to 1,500 feet, in the man-
ner which we had practiced for a month and had dis-
cussed for three additional weeks.

There was just time to get up there, level off, at-
tend to the routine of opening the bomb bay, make a
short run and let fly with the first bomb. The red light

blinked on my instrument board, and I knew the first 500-pounder had gone.

Our speed was picking up. The red light blinked again, and I knew Clever had let the second bomb go. Just as the light blinked, a black cloud appeared about 100 yards or so in front of us and rushed past at great speed. Two more appeared ahead of us, on about the line of our wingtips, and they too swept past. They had our altitude perfectly, but they were leading us too much.

The third red light flickered, and since we were now over a flimsy area in the southern part of the city, the fourth light blinked. That was the incendiary, which I knew would separate as soon as it hit the wind and that dozens of small fire bombs would molt from it.

The moment the fourth red light showed I put the nose of the Ruptured Duck into a deep dive. I had changed the course somewhat for the short run leading up to the dropping of the incendiary. Now, as I dived, I looked back and out. I got a quick, indelible vision of one of our 500-pounders as it hit our steel-smelter target. The plant seemed to puff out its walls and then subside and dissolve in a black-and-red cloud.

Our diving speed picked up to 350 miles an hour in less time than it takes to tell it, and up there in the front of the vibrating bomber I dimly wondered why the Japanese didn't throw up a wall of machine-gun fire. We would have had to fly right through it.

I flattened out over a long row of low buildings and homes and got the hell out of there. I felt satisfied about the steel-smelter and hoped the other bombs had done as well. There was no way of telling, but I was positive that Tokyo could have been damaged that day with a rock.

Our actual bombing operation, from the time the first one went until the dive, consumed not more than thirty seconds.

We were very low now, snaking back and forth, expecting a cloud of Zeros from moment to moment.

I pushed the inter-phone button and asked Clever if he were sure the bombs were all away.

"Sure," he said. McClure set our course due south. Thatcher, looking behind us, said that smoke was beginning to rise. I told him to watch out for planes and let me know when he wanted the turret.

I nosed down a railroad track on the outskirts of the city and passed a locomotive close enough to see the surprised face of the engineer. As I went by I could have kicked myself for not giving the locomotive's boiler a burst of our forward 30-calibre guns, then I remembered that we might have better use for the ammunition. A string of telephone wires shone like silver strands in the sunlight. It wasn't difficult to imagine the excited voices coursing over them, giving our direction to those waiting for us ahead.

It was McClure who spotted the six Japanese biplane pursuits, ugly black crates that look as slow as observation planes. They were flying well above us in close formation. We watched them, waiting for them to dive, and hoped that if they did so our extremely low altitude would cause enough of them to crash before they could pull out.

But the planes stayed where they were, and we were in no mood to go up there and fight them.

There was the gas to consider. All our auxiliary gas was gone now. We were starting in on the wing tanks. With the city behind us, I dropped the speed.

Presently we were out over water again, for the coastline of Honshu, the main island on which Tokyo is located, slants to the southwest. We were going due south because it was part of the plan to confuse possible pursuers and to keep from tipping off our eventual intention of swinging westward to China.

Thatcher now got a chance to use his guns, but not on a plane. A big yacht loomed up ahead of us and, figuring it must be armed, I told Thatcher to give it a burst. We went over it, lifted our nose to put the tail down and Thatcher sprayed its decks with our 50-calibre stingers.

Not much later, as we edged along about twenty feet over the water, I looked ahead and four or five miles immediately in front of us three Japanese cruisers appeared. They were coming our way, fast. They spotted us about the exact instant we spotted them. I looked down at the water a moment, gauging my clearance, and, when I looked up again, the three cruisers were turning with amazing precision, leaving big white wakes for tails, to face us broadside.

I wanted no part of them. I skirted deeply around them, and they didn't fire a shot.

McClure got us back on our course. Now, in line with the long-rehearsed plan, we altered our course to southwest. The island of Honshu has a lumpy, half-submerged tail of islands curling southwestwardly from it. Our marker was the volcanic mass named Yaku Shima which rises out of and forms a kind of eastern barrier of the China Sea.

We bored along our course through the long bright afternoon, all of us under considerable strain. Then, with a yell, we spotted what was unmistakably Yaku Shima and the smaller near-by Sumi Gunto. I flew between their wide-set gorge, held the course a bit longer, and then turned due west. We were now on the 29th parallel and winging out over the China Sea for our still-distant Choo Chow Lishui.

That broke the ice.

"Wow! What a headache I've got," Davenport said into the inter-phone.

I guess everybody had one. I told Thatcher to keep his eye peeled on the rear. I said that this thing wasn't over by a hell of a sight. He said he wasn't asleep.

We were flying so low and were so much on the lookout that once the plane edged toward the water when I looked up momentarily, and we came awful close to touching it. Our nerves twanged like guitar strings, so I told Davenport to do the looking around while I did the piloting, and, after about ten or fifteen minutes, we reversed the jobs.

We could smoke now, and that helped a lot. The extra gas, of course, was all out of the ship, so there was no danger from the cigarettes. Thatcher passed up some of the chocolate bars from the rear and we nibbled on them. But none of us had much of an appetite. Besides, they made us thirsty and we had no water. We had found one thermos bottle in the plane after the take-off but had finished it before we got to Tokyo.

We saw an occasional fishing boat or yacht in the China Sea as the afternoon wore along and figured that they were probably radioing ahead to Japanese-held airdromes on the China mainland, giving them our direction.

About five o'clock in the afternoon, when we were halfway across the China Sea, we spotted two submarines being refueled. They were tied up to a tanker. I wished we had saved a bomb. There didn't seem to be much good using our machine-gun ammunition on them, either. There would be plenty of uses for it over Japanese-held China, I thought. It was just impossible for me to believe that we were going to get away from the raid as easily as this.

Clever crawled up from his bombardier's nose and climbed into our compartment.

"Were you scared?" he asked me.

I told him I sure was.

I guess we all wanted to be together, now. We smoked a cigarette and talked as best we could, and I tried not to notice that the weather was going bad. The engines were wonderful. I felt like getting out on the wing and kissing them.

Local showers splattered our windshields. We had not expected good weather all the way. The Navy had warned us that this time of year often saw storms gather and roll off the shelf of China without much warning. I hoped this one wasn't going to get as bad as it promised. Finding Choo Chow Lishui without radio guidance would be a tough job under ideal weather conditions. Now it was beginning to be a terrific task.

Clever went back to his bombardier's nose and found out what was wrong with the automatic pilot. The improvised bomb sight—a rod of duralumin stuck downward at a tangent like the barrel of a rifle—had been fouling the gyroscopic action of the robot mechanism. The thing was soon working. That gave me my first chance to get up from my seat since about eight o'clock that morning. Davenport stayed in the co-pilot's seat, ready to grab the controls if anything went wrong with the automatic pilot, while I stepped down into McClure's navigation pit and stretched.

Thatcher saw me there and he crawled up. He seemed worried.

"What should I do if I have to bail out over water?" he asked me.

I told him we were going along all right and that there wasn't anything to worry about. But he wanted to know. So I told him that the thing to do was unfasten the leg straps as you came down, then, when you were eight or ten feet over the water to unhook the chest buckle of the chute and fall in the water. That would let the chute sail out of the way a little and it wouldn't come down on you and snarl you.

Then I asked him what made him think we'd bail out in water.

"I wasn't thinking so much about this," he said, pointing down. "I thought we might have to bail out over land and that I'd come down in a river or a lake."

There was one silver lining to the increasingly bad weather. If it kept up, our chances of being attacked by Japanese planes when we reached the Chinese coast would be pretty slim. And, after another hour, there wasn't much doubt that it would keep up. It was getting worse all the time. It was going to get dark early.

After I went back to the pilot's seat and relieved Davenport, I raised our nose up to about 500 feet and completely lost sight of the water. I came back down to fifty feet and the weather was getting so thick that now and then I'd have to roll back the window on my left and take a look out, for the windshield was clouding. Cigarettes had lost their taste now.

We sighted land at 8:30 P.M. on our watches, 6:30 local time. It was an eerie, peaked island that rose up out of the mist in front of us. I had to take the automatic pilot off presently because the worse the weather got the thicker the islands came. I'd fly blindly through clouds and squalls so thick that I could hardly see the nose of the ship. Once, one of the islands loomed up so close to us that I had to put the nose of the ship up in a hurry to keep from colliding. It got nerve-racking after that, flying blindly and hoping I'd see the islands in time to pull up.

There were two courses open now. I could continue what I was doing and stay low, looking for some memorized landmark or landing point, or I could climb, try to get above the storm and fly due west on instruments until the wing tanks gave out—then jump.

The latter course meant losing the plane. It meant too much to me. And it would mean a lot to the Chinese, too.

"Mainland!" somebody suddenly yelled in the inter-phone. I got a thick view of surf breaking over a beach, but all of us soon had our doubts. I asked McClure what he thought, after it was obvious that this was just another island.

"I think we ought to go a little farther south," he said. "It must be all occupied along here. I can't tell much about anything, with this visibility."

I flew south, very low, for about ten minutes. Then McClure said, "I don't think we'll ever find anything this way." That made up my mind. I decided to go up and fly in on instruments, but it hurt me to think of losing the plane. Choo Chow Lishui is about 100 miles inland. Even if we found it, it would be unlighted. We wouldn't know whether it had been occupied or not, for we needed light to see the Chinese signal. But it seemed like the only thing to do.

I made three big circles, gaining altitude without using too much gas. At 500 feet we suddenly ran into a clear hole in the weather. Davenport yelled and pointed down. There below us in the dusk was a clean, concave beach. Land extended as far as we could see in the hole in the weather. It looked durable, with a strong suggestion of mainland.

I had to make up my mind in a hurry. The thing to do, I decided, was see if I could get down on the beach. If I could, we'd spend the night in the plane, take off at dawn and find Choo Chow Lishui in the daylight. I had a little over a hundred gallons of gas left.

Landing here and now meant something else to me, more than the thought of capture. It's hard and embarrassing to speak of love for a plane, but I loved that ship. To desert it in the air, coughing and preparing to nose over for its final plunge, was beyond endurance.

I dropped down low and dragged the beach, inspecting it for logs. The sand was wet from the rain that was pounding down, but it looked firm enough to support that touchy nose wheel of ours. There were no logs to tear the underpinning off us. It was by all means the best thing I had seen for twelve hours or more.

So I spoke into the inter-phone and told the boys we were going down. I told them to take off their chutes, but didn't have time to take off mine, and to be sure their life jackets were on, as mine was. I put the flaps down and also the landing wheels, and I remember thinking momentarily that if this was Japanese-occupied land we could make a pretty good fight of it while we lasted. Our front machine gun was detachable.

McClure placed our .45's and their holsters behind our seats. The .25 Ellen had given me was in my shoulder holster, under my shirt. McClure now came up from his navigating well and knelt behind our pilot seats, sticking his head between us and bracing his shoulders against our back rests.

The concave shape of the beach meant that I would have to come into it over water and make a slight turn before putting the plane down.

Davenport was calling off the airspeed. He had just said, "One hundred and ten," when, for some reason I'll never understand, both engines coughed and lost their power.

In the next split second my hands punched forward and with one motion I hit both throttles, trying to force life back into the engines, and both prop pitch controls. And I tried to pull back the stick to keep the nose up, so we could squash in. We were about a quarter of a mile off-shore when we hit.

The two main landing wheels caught the top of a wave as the plane sagged. And the curse of desperation and disappointment that I instinctively uttered was drowned out by the most terrifying noise I ever heard.

It was as if some great hand had reached down through the storm, seized the plane and crunched it in a closing fist.

Then nothing. Nothing but peace. A strange, strange, peaceful feeling. There wasn't any pain. A great, restful quiet surrounded me.

Then I must have swallowed some water, or perhaps the initial shock was wearing off, for I realized vaguely but inescapably that I was sitting in my pilot's seat on the sand, under water.

I was in about ten or fifteen feet of water, I sensed remotely. I remember thinking: I'm dead. Then: No, I'm just hurt. Hurt bad. I couldn't move, but there was no feeling of being trapped, or of fighting for air.

I thought then of Ellen—strange thoughts filled with vague reasoning but little torment. A growing uneasiness came through my numb body. I wished I had left Ellen some money. I thought of money for my mother, too, in those disembodied seconds that seemed to have no beginning or end.

I guess I must have taken in more water, for suddenly I knew that the silence, the peace and the reverie were things to fight against. I could not feel my arms, yet I knew I reached down and unbuckled the seat strap that was holding me to the chair. I told myself that my guts were loose.

I drifted up off the seat and started to the surface. It was like a dream of trying to escape from something that moves very swiftly, while you move slowly. There was no power in my arms or legs, only an instinctive want to live—a want that I couldn't understand. It didn't seem possible to hold the water out of me even one more second.

My pneumatic lifebelt brought me to the surface. Through some streak of luck the shock of being thrown out of the plane in the crash had broken the dioxide capsule that inflates the belt.

I came up into the driving rain that beat down out of the blackening sky. I couldn't swim. I was paralyzed. I couldn't think clearly, but I undid my chute.

The waves lifted me and dropped me. One wave washed me against a solid object, and, after I had stared at it in the gloom for a while, I realized that it was one of the wings of the plane. I noticed that the engine had been ripped off the wing, leaving only a tangle of broken wire and cable. And with the recognition came a surge of nausea and despair, for only now did I connect my condition with the condition of the plane.

Another wave took me away from the wing and when it turned me around I saw behind me the two tail rudders of the ship, sticking up out of the water like twin tombstones.

The waves had brought me in now to the point where they were breaking. I struggled feebly against them, but they'd lift me up and pull me under with their punishing roar in my ears and I'd roll around on the bottom until my belt brought me to the top again.

Once I felt the slipping sand of the beach's edge under me. I tried to crawl up out of the water but the suction of a returning wave pulled me in again. This happened several times. But then one wave carried me so far in that I crawled up on the beach out of their reach.

I stood up. My legs felt numb. I thought that if I walked around a little bit it would bring circulation back to them. So I walked around in circles on the beach in the rain.

I was the only one on the beach. That didn't impress me much when I first thought of it. When I did comprehend what it meant I started to curse in a muffled voice I couldn't recognize. I cursed myself for the loss of my men and the loss of that ship.

My voice sounded so strange to me, and the words came so thickly, that I vaguely reached up to my mouth and felt it. The bottom lip had been cut through and torn down to the cleft of my chin, so that the skin flapped over and down. My upper teeth were bent in. I reached into my mouth with both of my thumbs and put my thumbs behind the teeth and tried to push them out straight again. They bent out straight, then broke off in my hands. I did the same with the bottom teeth and they broke off too, bringing with them pieces of my lower gum.

I stood in the rain with that wet handful of teeth and gum for a while, trying to think. Then I dropped the stuff on the beach. I guess I must have been punch-drunk because I remember saying to myself that now I'd have to go to a dentist.

For some reason I can't explain I started to stagger up the beach. I didn't know where I was going. After a bit I thought I heard someone behind me and when I looked around there was Davenport walking toward me.

Davenport came up to me. We didn't say anything. He took my head in his hands and held it back so he could see it a little better. I tried to say how glad I was to see him, but he said, "God damn! You're really bashed open. Your whole face is pushed in."

What he said meant nothing. I was looking at the blood running down his forehead from his head. I asked him mushily if he was hurt bad.

"I think so," Davenport said. "I don't know."

Speaking, and the sight of each other, seemed to bring us farther along toward complete consciousness, and both of us began to moan, standing there next to each other in the black rain.

Then Davenport wandered away from me and began calling, "Hey! Hey!" I couldn't understand it, and I guess he couldn't understand it himself.

I turned around again and there were two men on the beach. I could hear someone else flopping in the water. I stumbled up to the first one. It was McClure. He was dazed and groaning. I looked him all over. He had some cuts, but they didn't seem bad.

I went over to Clever. He was in the sand on his hands and knees with his head hanging down between his arms. He didn't crawl and he couldn't speak. When the waves would come in they would flow around him a few inches deep and then go out again, so that his knees and his hands sank down a little in the slipping sand. When the water was in you could hear the blood that was pouring from his face and head fall into the water.

I tried to pick up Clever. Finally the two of us stumbled up on the beach. He walked a few feet and fell down on his hands and knees again. He didn't even moan. I turned around, looking for somebody to help me with him, and there was Thatcher walking up out of the water.

Thatcher had a bleeding bump on his head, but he seemed all right.

We all got together now on the beach, near where Clever was on his hands and knees, bleeding terribly. It was very dark now and the rain was getting heavier. I kept trying to think straight, but all I was able to do was moan. Davenport began to call "Hey!" again. Thatcher, McClure and I called with him. I guess the noise must have aroused Clever, for he looked up as if he didn't recognize any of us. He struggled to his feet, tried to walk and fell down again on all fours.

I decided to build a fire. I was out of my head. Very plainly in my scrambled brain I could see hundreds of square flat boards, nice and dry, spread all around the beach. A fire would be best for us, I said. We were all shivering. There was a tiny cliff rising four or five feet at the back of the beach. I saw myself collecting the square, dry boards, stacking them against the cliff and lighting the fire.

We must have lain there in the rain on the beach

for half an hour, trying to talk. Then, as if I were still dreaming, I saw Thatcher do a strange thing. He was the only one who had saved his .45. Now he reached into his holster, got it out and aimed it up over my head. I just watched him.

"Shall I shoot them, Lieutenant?" Thatcher asked me.

I rolled over, to look. Two men were standing on the top of the little cliff, staring silently down at us.

They were strong, squat-looking men, bundled up in some sort of coat that shone almost like a raincoat. They had on flat, woven hats. We looked at them. I told Thatcher not to shoot. I don't know why I said it.

"Hey!" Davenport called.

Cautiously the men stepped down the embankment and walked over to us. I tried to study their faces, but it was too dark. I had enough sense now to experience some distantly alarming feeling that these might be Japanese. But it wouldn't have made much difference, then.

The men went from one of us to the other, peering at our wounds and humming. "Hmmmmm. Hmmmmmm." That's the only way I can spell it. It was half mournful, half incredulous. We just stood there or lay there, too broken up to do anything about it.

Six more men now ran down the embankment. They examined us very carefully and hummed.

Then one of them looked at me. He touched his chest, simply.

"Chinga," he said.

We had been found by Chinese.

They bombarded us suddenly with many questions in Chinese, and that made us remember a Chinese phrase we had memorized during the last week of our training.

"Lishua Megwa, Lishua Megwa," we babbled. They nodded. Roughly, it is Chinese for an American.

One of them now counted us elaborately on his fingers. Then he pointed toward where the plane rested, counted five on his fingers, then paused, ready to count more.

We told him by gesture and counting that there were no more men in the plane. It took some time, but at last they understood.

They helped us up now, the rain running off their wide hats when they bent over us. McClure let out a terrible scream when two of them took him under the armpits and lifted him. They dropped him again. Mc-Clure got up by himself and made a show of walking along. "I think my shoulders are broken," he said. "I hit the backs of your seats."

Two of them carried Clever, two of them braced me and we went up the beach a few yards to a point where the embankment ended. The Chinese led us along a rude, narrow path, our feet slipping in the mud, the wet leaves brushing over us. It was wholly unreal.

We followed the path for several hundred yards, moaning. It was an ordeal that brought my reasoning back a little more. I had a burst of fear because I now vividly remembered something that had been pounded into us during the lectures. We had been told that there were many places along the coast of China where the Japanese had installed puppet governments; that Chinese in power in these areas sometimes sold information to the Japanese. I had no idea where these men were taking us, and though later it made me ashamed to think that I had mistrusted them, that night I wouldn't have been surprised if they had carried us to the Japanese.

They took us up to a low, thatched-roof house which we didn't see until we were within a few yards of it. It was made of mud blocks. It was rectangular in shape with a door in the center and a dim light shining from it. We fell into the place, mangled and moaning.

It had a dirt floor and, by the smoky light of a lamp, I could see it was roughly divided into two rooms. In the far right-hand corner of the larger room was a low bed made of rawhide strips stretched over a kind of cot structure. Davenport, Thatcher and I sat down on the bed, our backs to the mud-brick wall. McClure tried to lie down across the room from us, but he screamed again when he stretched out. So he pulled himself up against the wall, propped himself against it in a sitting position and asked Thatcher to put something behind his back.

Poor Clever had not said a word. He was bleeding terribly. He crawled over to the corner opposite us and passed out in a mound of human dung, his bleeding face resting against it. We hadn't enough strength then to pull him off. The Chinese didn't seem to think it unusual.

The lamp gave off more smoke than light, but there was enough light to see two Chinese women moving about in the other room. They were dressed in rough-looking pants, with a short, skirt-like robe to the knee. One of them came up to us on the bed and handed us a quilt of some unfinished material. We spread it out over us, for now we were trembling with cold as well as with pain.

When I warmed up a bit, and I knew for sure that this was no frightening nightmare, I told myself that it was time to see just what had happened to me. I pushed the quilt aside and, with the help of the Chinese men, I got out of what was left of my pants. I had no idea that there would be anything wrong with my left leg except a bruise. It was cut from my upper thigh to my knee, and cut so deeply that it lay open widely enough so that I looked into it and saw the gristle and muscle and bone.

It wasn't bleeding badly—just oozing. My circulation probably had slowed down because of the shock and the cold. I just stared at it, hypnotized and detached. I had never seen anything like it.

Most of my shirt was torn off, so I began to get out of the rest of it. The Chinese men helping me let out a low hum. I looked up at them and saw one pointing to my left arm. The biceps, halfway between my elbow and shoulder, had been cut as cleanly as if by an axe. The biceps had ripped downward until it lay in the crook of my arm. I didn't even know it was hurt.

The others, except Clever, were undressing also. We looked ourselves over first, then turned our attention to one another. Davenport kept looking at me and finally he said, "Jesus, Lawson, your face looks terrible! How do you feel?" There wasn't anything to say. The Chinese men and women kept moving among us, speaking softly. There was little or no change in their worn faces, but there was in the sound of their voices. They kept saying, "Hmmmmmm."

I looked through my torn clothes to see what was left. My shoulder holster with Ellen's gun had stayed on me. My wallet was also in my trousers. I opened it now and water ran out of it. I took out Ellen's picture and examined it. I went through the rest of my wallet and found $14, some stuck-together three-cent stamps, my California driver's license, social security card, private pilot's license and a filled-out form listing my blood type and the immunizing shots I had taken for this trip. I looked at all these things as if I were examining a billfold I had just found. I handed Ellen's gun to Thatcher and told him to hide it.

One of the Chinese was standing over me, watching me. I looked at him, pointed to the gash in my leg and made a sewing motion over the wound. I said the word needle and the word thread. He shook his head but called one of the others over. I did the same thing, but they shook their heads. They either had no needle and thread or they were hesitant to let me use it to sew my leg together again.

Outside, the rain was thumping down, but above the noise of it I heard someone coming. Pretty soon an amazing-looking man appeared in the faintly lighted doorway. He had one of the strongest faces I've ever seen. He wasn't a big man, but he gave the impression of enormous strength. His immobile face was an iron mask of determination.

His black eyes, set in that muscular dead-pan,

darted around the room. Then he stepped forward briskly and went from one of us to the other, looking at our wounds and closely and suspiciously examining all buttons, insignia and other identifying markings left on our torn clothes.

He was dressed in an old pair of American-looking pants, heavy shoes, a thick hunting shirt, open at the neck, and wore no hat. His wet hair was pitch black and coarsely combed. The Chinese showed him quiet deference.

When he completed his inspection of the room he spoke for a minute or two to a tall man who had accompanied him. He looked at us without a sign of pity in his inscrutable face. I just looked back at his stony face, wondering if he was planning to sell us.

Then he came up to me and stood there looking down at my mashed face.

"Me—Charlie," he said.

I couldn't believe my ears until he said it again, solemnly.

We broke out in a rash of garbled questions. Where were we? Could we get to Choo Chow Lishui in a hurry? Where was the nearest doctor? Would Charlie help us? We had money. . . .

Charlie stood there and stared back at me. If he showed any expression at all it was one of impatience.

"Me—Charlie," he repeated.

"Lishua Megwa," Davenport said, pointing to us. Charlie stared. Then we all tried to pronounce it. Charlie finally nodded briefly, without expression.

"Melican," he stated.

"Yes, yes, yes," we all said, so animatedly that McClure moved out of the one comfortable position he had found and had to yell for help to get back in it, the pain was so great. Poor Clever just lay there in the corner, his face oozing into the piled excrement. We flooded Charlie with questions, our voices finally trailing off when we realized that he didn't understand.

Davenport started from the beginning again. "Lishua Megwa," he said, and added, "Oh, God."

"Melican," Charlie returned.

We all tried different pronunciations of Choo Chow Lishui. Charlie shook his head.

"Chiang Kai-shek," we said, thickly. "Chiang Kai-shek—we're friends."

It was hopeless no matter how we pronounced it. "Generallissimo" didn't help, either.

"Chungking," Davenport said.

Charlie nodded. "Chungking," he repeated, almost as Davenport had.

"Chungking . . . We go, go."

Charlie didn't move. "Chungking—many—many day. Many."

"How many?" I counted off numbers on my fingers, which I noticed only then were cut.

"Many day," Charlie said, shaking his head.

For at least an hour we tried to find out how many days. We got hopelessly mixed up in days, hours, miles and li. The li is a Chinese measure, roughly a third of a mile. We'd say something about days and Charlie would think we meant li, or miles.

"Doc-tor," we said. Charlie understood.

"Doc-tor," he repeated. Then held up three fingers and added, "Day."

Three days! We needed one this instant, for the shock was beginning to wear off all of us, except Clever. I thought of the medicine kit in the plane and now I sent Thatcher—who was in the best condition—back to the beach to see if he could get to the plane and find it.

"Charlie go doc-tor," Davenport said, pointing to him. "Charlie bring doc-tor here—maybe one day—two day?" We said it as many ways as we could, until Charlie understood.

He shook his head. We were afraid to believe what our new-found knowledge of pidgin-English and gesture-language was telling us.

I pointed to Clever, at the cuts on Davenport, at McClure's jammed-down shoulders and at my leg and arm and mouth. And begged him to bring a doctor.

Charlie shook his head a little impatiently, dismissing the thought. He stared at us impassively for a while. Then he said, "Doc-tor—one li."

One li! He had said three days before that. We tried to tell him something was wrong.

"Doc-tor—one li," he insisted.

"Bring doc-tor, one li."

Again he shook his head and before we could cry out in anguish he said, "Doc-tor, one li, Japanee man. Japanee doc-tor."

The word came down heavily on us in the smoky room.

"Maybe Japanee men—Japanee soldier—catch us," we said to Charlie.

Charlie comprehended, and, for the first time during the whole painful meeting, the trace of a smile touched the corners of his hard mouth.

"Japanee man," Charlie said, "no come out at night." He said it with his teeth set—a hard, fighting glint in his eyes.

Thatcher came back about this time and our worst fears about our stuff in the plane were realized. "I couldn't even see the plane," he said. "The tide seems to have come in and covered it—and there wasn't anything washed up on the beach."

I could feel his words in every one of my cuts and I guess the others could, too.

One of the Chinese women, the one who had given us the now-bloody quilt, brought in some hot water in small bowls and in earthen pots. We drank some of it and washed some of the blood off us. With the help of the Chinese we got the unconscious Clever onto a mat and covered him. None of us had any desire for food, though we had had none since supper the evening of the 17th. Now it was two or three o'clock in the morning of Sunday, the 19th.

We talked nearly all that night to Charlie, and, when we weren't talking to him, we mumbled among ourselves or just moaned as the shock continued to wear off and the pains became worse. Charlie again inspected every article of clothing we had with us. Then he left, after another hour of words and gestures had told us that he would come back soon. He said "Boat" many times.

We talked about him for a while, wondering who he was and what our chances were. We decided that the Chinese who had found us on the beach were fishermen and that Charlie was some kind of official.

And we talked about the crash. I came to what

must be the only answer, for I've never found another. When the wheels caught the top of that wave, as we came in toward the beach, the plane stopped as if it had hit a solid wall at 110 mph. That shock, plus the weight of McClure being thrown against the back of my seat, ripped the seat up by its roots and catapulted me—I was strapped in—through the glass, plastic and metal windshield.

I decided then, and still believe, that my leg was laid open as I shot past and scraped along the left side of the pilot's compartment. The leg evidently grabbed the metal clip on which we stick our earphones.

The same thing happened to Davenport, he said, after I had mumbled my version. But he went through cleaner than I did. Clever, we found out later, was crawling back through the narrow tunnel leading from the bombardier's section in the nose of the plane when we hit. He shot forward and through the transparent, metal-braced nose like a man shot out of a cannon.

McClure stayed in the plane because much of the catapulting force must have been spent on the backs of our seats. But as Mac sat there propped against the wall of the fisherman's hut, aching and knowing that some kind of Japanese detachment was near by, he couldn't remember how he got out of the plane.

Thatcher said he bounced around in the back like

a pea in a drum. Unlike the rest of us, he had dressed in heavy clothes the morning we took off. That saved him. He was knocked out for a little time, regained consciousness with water in the plane and got out an emergency exit. He said the plane was upside down.

I began to shake with the cold. The quilt had turned icy. I pulled it away from where it was sticking to my leg and saw that the blood had been coming out faster, hitting the quilt, seeping through it and then cooling off in the night air that filled the room. Outside, the rain came down hard. It would have been easier just to shut my eyes and pass out. But whenever I did I remembered my cuts. And the unspeakable pain.

I asked Thatcher for his roll of bandage and wrapped it around my leg cut. Our rolls of bandage had been ripped off our provision belts, along with everything else. Then I took my trouser belt, put it around the bandage on my thigh and pulled up on it as tightly as I could. It just closed the middle part of the gash. The two ends sagged open. I loosened the belt and tried it down a little farther, then tied my necktie around the upper part. Thatcher ripped off a piece of my torn shirt and we tied my torn biceps back in place.

I wondered all the time whether Charlie would come back, and, if he did come back, whether he'd bring Japanese.

Just before dawn on the morning of the 19th an elderly Chinese appeared in the doorway and came in. He looked me over from head to foot, but seemed most interested in my mouth. Finally he fumbled in his loose pockets, drew out something and gently pushed my head back until I looked up at the dim, thatched ceiling. He put a piece of what looked like rice paper over my mouth, after fitting the torn flesh in more or less the place it belonged. When the blood soaked through the paper he sprinkled some powdered matter on the places where the blood came through. He didn't say a word, nor did I. To this day I cannot say who he was, where he came from and what he did to me. Charlie must have sent him.

The blood, powder and paper formed a kind of crude plaster that kept my mouth in shape and stopped a lot of its bleeding the rest of the night.

Only Clever slept. The rest of us sat there or lay there under the soaked cover, waiting. Our aches, the enormity of the problem of getting away from here, and the Japanese, were on our minds. Sometimes McClure called to Thatcher to help him. Nearly every position McClure assumed was excruciating. Sometimes Davenport talked to McClure and Thatcher. I couldn't speak now. But I could listen, and I could hope that Charlie would come back.

When McClure asked me if I trusted Charlie, I nodded that I did.

After an overpowering eternity, the gray, cold, rainy dawn filtered into the room like a ghost. I shifted the plaster a little and told Thatcher to go down to the beach again, locate the plane, get what he could out of it and pick up whatever had drifted in. Thatcher looked at me a moment and I could tell he was thinking about his chances of being captured. But he said, "Yes, sir," and went out. I don't know what we would have done without Thatcher.

As it grew lighter the Chinese stirred. At the first clatter of pottery in the other room I heard the sleepy voices of children. Soon they ran into our room. There were three of them, the oldest about five, I'd say. They marched right up and stared at our cuts and bruises, sometimes reaching out to touch them gingerly. They fingered our clothes and buttons. A Chinese woman I hadn't seen the night before came in, looked at us and sighed.

I wanted to give them something. I had lost all the coins. I looked across the room where McClure was shaking the loose insides of his watch near the ear of one of the children. I thought of my own watches for the first time and realized only then that they had both been torn off my wrists. I gave the children a shredded leather jacket and some buttons, and when they went out of the room I thought about the watches again—the Elgin my mother had given me when I graduated from high school and the navigator's hack watch with the sweep second hand.

I thought of Ellen, too. I wondered if she could sense what had happened.

The noise of the children woke up Clever. He groaned and turned over. His face was a hard mask of stiff blood. Davenport called for some water. I worked my mouth plaster around some more and said something to Clever as he stirred.

Clever opened his eyes. It must have been an effort, with the blood caked all around the lids. He looked slowly all around the room, and then at us. "I thought I was blind," he said. Then very quietly he asked where we were, what had happened, whether we were going to get away. He was silent after that, but just looking at him made all of us begin to hurt more and we were moaning without shame when Thatcher came back.

Thatcher was wringing wet. In his hand he had a carton of cigarettes and a lifebelt.

"I got to the plane, all right," he said to me. "But this is all I could find. I couldn't get down in the forward part—only in the tail. It's sticking up again on account of low tide."

The cigarettes weren't much of a substitute for the morphine and iodine I had been trying not to think about. But they helped. We peeled the cellophane off them and they burned, even though they were very damp.

Charlie came back about seven o'clock that morning. With him he brought a number of ragged, docile Chinese men. I could see them through the door, standing miserably in the rain. Some of them carried stout bamboo poles about ten feet long. Others carried ropes. They seemed to be reluctant to do what Charlie was ordering them to do. But when they spoke back to him, complainingly or stubbornly, his strong voice rose above their voices indignantly.

Now I saw other coolies, if that is what these men were, carrying four flat lattice-work squares. They were about three-by-three and something like a grating. To the four corners of each crude square stretcher—for that's about the best way to describe it—I saw Charlie and one of his lieutenants tie the short ropes. It was agonizingly slow work. The thought that the delay might result in our capture was intolerable. I yelled out to Charlie thickly and told him I could help with the knots, for the Navy boys had showed me things I didn't know could be done with a rope.

Charlie ignored me. The important thing, I kept

telling myself, was that Charlie had not only come back but was obviously planning to have us carried away.

About three hours after they began work, the Chinese had the litters ready. They slipped a bamboo pole through the joined ends of the ropes on the last square stretcher, made it fast, and Charlie beckoned for one of us to come out.

McClure got painfully to his feet, tried to stretch without hurting his shoulders and walked stiffly to where his short, square stretcher swayed between two Chinese. Each had an end of the pole on his shoulder. Charlie made motions to McClure to get up on the stretcher, sit up and hold onto the ropes for support.

It was tough on McClure, with those shoulders. He couldn't raise his arms more than a few inches. But he finally made it, after nearly tipping over, and hung onto the back ropes near where they were tied to the corners of the carrier. Charlie jabbered at the coolies and they shuffled off down the narrow path that led away from the fisherman's hut.

The Chinese helped Clever out next, then Davenport. And carried them away. McClure had been gone about an hour and a half before my time came. They brought my stretcher into the house. A couple of them held me while I got up and tried to walk, but I couldn't help myself up on the carrier. I pulled the plaster on my mouth down a little more so I could enunciate better and ask them to lower the platform to the dirt floor. I wanted just to drop down on it. They couldn't understand me. When I pushed down on the side of the stretcher and looked pleadingly at them, I guess they thought I was just testing the strength of the thing.

Finally they got it. I half rolled on it as it touched the ground and lay there, moaning. When they lifted it, my numb lower legs dangled over the front end and I held on to the rear ropes.

Just as they lifted me there was a commotion outside. The men who were to carry me put me down on the floor again and ran out. I lay there about fifteen minutes before asking Thatcher to go outside and see what the trouble was. He came back and said, "I can't make head nor tail of it. It's just jabbering."

It was cold on the dirt floor. The only clothes I had on were my shorts. I crawled across the floor to the bed, pulled myself up on it and drew the stiff, blood-crusted quilt up around me. And I moaned. I just couldn't help it.

The woman who had loaned me the quilt now came back in the room, looked at its condition and snatched it off me, holding it up and examining it. She made small, impatient, clucking noises. I didn't know what to say. I had my money and I offered her some bills and reached for the quilt. But I don't think she recognized the money. One of my shoes had been torn off when I went through the windshield, but I had gotten there with the other one. I offered it to her, feeling pretty foolish, for I had made a terrible mess of her quilt. She examined the shoe closely. Finally she took it and the lifebelt Thatcher had brought back from the plane, and handed the quilt back to me.

After another fifteen minutes, Charlie led the two coolies back into the room. They got me back on the stretcher and carried me out. I don't think I cared much where they were taking me, by that time. It must have been about noon.

The weather was beginning to clear as we left the winding path away from the fisherman's place and threaded our way along the overgrown path. Thatcher was walking behind me. I was carried off the path and along the little dykes of rice paddies. We were going up to higher ground, and I thought I might get a glimpse of the plane. I twisted around as much as I could on my cramped conveyance, and asked Thatcher also to look down toward the beach. But we couldn't see what was left of the Ruptured Duck. Somehow I was glad I couldn't.

The coolies stopped at a little farm where a Chinese in a broad straw hat was working in a field and chatted animatedly with him, looking now and then at me. The Chinese carrying the front end of the pole was very young and much stronger than the ancient man behind me. None of the coolies wore hats. They were covered with short pants made of coarse gray material—apparently hand-woven—had on open shirts and were barefooted. Their feet were big, flat and sure. As we rose to still higher ground, the men climbed mossy rocks as if they were steps. Their toes gripped the rocks like fingers. I hung on as I swung between them like a butchered hog.

It must have been in the early afternoon of the 19th when we reached the top of the hill we had been climbing, passed through a weird natural tunnel and came out of it to look down on a verdant valley. We passed down a narrow trail that was lined with tall brambly bushes, something like berry bushes. The trail was widening. I half raised myself and looked ahead.

A big, lush meadow stretched out before me. There was a rather large, comparatively modern house to the left. In front of it were McClure, Davenport and Clever. There were some stunted, starved-looking Chinese cattle grazing near by.

But what held my eye was that about 200 tough-looking, sinister men stood here and there about the house, silently watching us come toward them. I could see even from a distance that they were well armed. I had to blink. It seemed so unreal. I thought of some half-remembered, half-scrambled impression of Robin Hood. It must have been the way several of the waiting men stood poised on the edge of a neighboring woods—tense, watchful.

I was glad when I spotted Charlie near the house. He still might be turning us in, but at least I seemed to derive some strength and determination just from the sight of his strong, almost cruel face. He was obviously in charge here. All remaining doubt that he was a guer-rilla began to flee my mind.

My coolies put me down near Clever in front of the house. Charlie hovered over us as some of Charlie's men edged in closer, squatted on their haunches in a circle and looked at us.

"You—eat?" Charlie asked me.

If I nodded my head negatively, which to me would have meant that I had not eaten, he might think I was declining food. So I just pointed to what was left of my mouth, and so did the others.

For some reason—probably our bloody condi-tion—they wouldn't take us inside. I could see that the place was clean and had a floor. Charlie disappeared and we were left with the staring circle of guerrillas. We studied their tough, weather-beaten faces as intently as they studied our wounds. I wondered if all of them could resist the temptation to turn us over to the Japanese. The Japanese must want us badly enough to pay a lot, I thought.

One of the toughest-looking men in the bunch now got up and advanced on me as I lay there, too exhausted from the trip over the hill to care what he would do to me. He reached down quickly toward my mouth and when he pulled his hand away I felt a lighted cigarette between that part of my lips which still met.

I tried to smile back at him, but I felt more like crying. Maybe from relief. Maybe shock. I don't know. Anyway, I closed my eyes now and I thought that wherever I was I was among good men—men who were fighting for about the same thing I was fighting for. These men had us at their mercy, and showed us that mercy. I remember mumbling to myself that if I could stay here, and get well, it would be good. I wanted to go on fighting, with them.

I opened my eyes again when Charlie reappeared carrying bowls of some sickly gray stuff, covered with a rough sauce that looked alive. None of us had now eaten anything since the early evening of the 17th.

But the thought of trying to get it down my throat was too much for me. I had to say no. I finally got the idea over to Charlie that I wanted hot water. So did the others. We had heard so many lectures about the dangers of drinking un-boiled water, in case we had to land or jump before we reached the pre-ordained fields, that it stuck in our heads even under these circumstances.

Charlie went back in and returned soon with bowls of hot water with a deep Chinese spoon in each. The guerrillas watched us gulp it. The new ones who came up would stare at my face a long time and, invariably, cluck their tongues. I wondered if they knew what we had done. Charlie must, though we had told nothing.

When we were finished with the hot water, Charlie reached over and started to take the .45 or Ellen's .25 out of the two holsters Thatcher wore. Thatcher was very proud of his .45 and I had asked him to take good care of Ellen's .25. So he wrenched away from Charlie, while a sudden murmur of disapproval buzzed up from the guerrillas.

It was a bad moment, but Charlie looked more surprised than hurt. I got us over the impasse accidentally. I said, in pidgin-English, that we needed the guns to shoot Japanese. I told him anxiously that there were machine guns in the plane and he could have them. To get over the idea of machine guns I held up my arms as a kid does, when he's making believe he's shooting one, and I made that aa-aa-aa-aa-aa-aa noise that kids make.

The guerrillas giggled, but Charlie was forbiddingly silent.

"Aa-aa-aa-aa-aa-aa — is *bent!*" he said with finality, and to make his amazing declaration clearer he made a motion of bending metal with his strong, brown hands. He was telling us, in effect, that his men had given the plane a pretty good frisk.

I should have thought of the medicine kit now and tried to get Charlie to send one of his men back to see if he could dive for it. But I guess I was too punchy by that time. Besides, we had another distraction. As if to bear out Charlie's hint that the plane had been inspected, one of the guerrillas walked past with one of our leather jackets. A coolie then marched in carrying a pole on whose ends were slung two baskets of twisted remains of our personal effects.

"Well I'll be a——," McClure said. "Hey! Have you got my camera?" he yelled after the coolie. We found out that it wasn't among the stuff salvaged. The loss of the camera was a blow to McClure. He had gotten what must have been a wonderful picture record of the raid from the time we started until the weather turned bad in the late afternoon. In fact, it was over Japan that I looked back once and saw him taking a shot and I yelled into the inter-phone and asked him what the hell he thought this was—a Cook's Tour?

From time to time as we lay there in front of the house of the guerrillas, armed Chinese would trot up and report to Charlie. After three or four had done so, Charlie unwound his English words and, with the aid of gestures, told us to go to sleep. We would continue the journey after dark, he made us understand, without telling us why.

I didn't go to sleep. I passed out, for by now everything on me was unbearable.

That was the last time I ever saw Charlie.

I came to in about an hour. The sun was still high. What woke me up was that I was being carried out of the meadow. I sensed a hurried change in Charlie's plans, but he was nowhere in sight to explain.

I had a feeling as I was carried out of the meadow that all of China was reaching out a hand to help us; that in some inscrutable way the word had been passed from heart to heart; that behind each impassive mask the secret of what we had done on the raid fairly sizzled. At least it seemed that way.

Six guerrillas, armed with rifles, marched beside our stretchers as we left the meadow. In half an hour or so we passed a tiny village, most of whose people lined up along the pathway. It was hot, and I had thrown off the stiff quilt, and now the villagers walked along beside my stretcher and the women cried, "Hmmmmmm. Hmmmmmm." The coolies who carried Clever stopped a moment and some of the Chinese women dropped on their knees at his side, repeating that humming wail or crying "Yi-yi-yi-yi . . ."

I tried to pull my flying wings off the piece of shirt beside me. I wanted to give something to these people. But I was carried on beyond the tiny village before I could.

Late on that afternoon of the 19th we reached the bank of a shallow, narrow canal just as a boatman poled a flat-bottom boat down the muddy water to the point where our path reached the water. I marveled dully at the timing of the meeting. The coolies lifted our stretchers into the boat. Four of the six armed guards jumped in after us as the boatman, sweating under his big straw hat, poled us out in the middle of the dirty canal and we headed slowly south. Our coolies stayed behind, wordlessly watching us.

We lay in the bottom of the boat, looking up at the blue dome of the perfect afternoon. After a while one of the guerrillas reached out toward Thatcher's .45, and I heard Thatcher say, "Cut it out!" But the guerrilla

didn't want the gun. He had a good German-type automatic, as well as his rifle. It developed that he wanted
only to exchange one of his bullets for one of
Thatcher's.

It was hard not to moan incessantly now, even
though the warm sun felt good. We passed slowly down
the canal for a couple of hours, the only sound being
the thump of the pole against the back of the boat and
an occasional jumble of conversation from the guerrillas. Sometimes the canal became so narrow that we
could have reached out and touched the sides. Sometimes the limbs of overgrowing trees made the silent
boatman bend low. I just lay there, hurting, and wondering what lay at the end of this ride and how I'd ever
be able to walk when the ride did end. Thatcher was
the only one of us who could walk.

The boatman steered us over to the side of the
canal, about five or six o'clock that afternoon. Two
steep dykes shut off our view. There was no landing
foothold. We waited, and in a very few minutes eight
new coolies came over the dyke and down the side to
the boat. Without a word of instruction they went to
our stretchers, picked us up and started up the dyke,
while we hung on miserably and wondered.

It was only when I got to the top of the dyke that I
realized that we were on an island, not the mainland of

Bob Considine (l.) and Capt. Ted Lawson in a discussion in front of the U.S. Capitol, probably in 1943. Mrs. Ellen R. Lawson

Cadet Ted Lawson over Randolph Field, San Antonio, Texas, in 1940. He is flying a North American BC-1A, the prewar designation of the famed AT-6 Texan advanced trainer. Mrs. Ellen R. Lawson

Cadet Lawson in the cockpit of his BC-1A in 1940. Mrs. Ellen R. Lawson

On February 1, 1942, on the day of the Navy's successful raid on the Marshall Islands, Admiral William F. Halsey, Jr. (center), and his staff pose for a group photo on the signal bridge of his flagship, USS Enterprise. *Halsey commanded Task Force 16 during the raid on Tokyo and made the decision to launch the Raiders early.* National Archives

Douglas TBD Devastators torpedo planes on board USS Enterprise during its escort of the Hornet toward Japan. These aircraft and their crews of VT-6 had seen action during February and March in raids on the Marshall Islands, but would face their greatest test during the Battle of Midway less than two months later. TBDs No. 7 and No. 8 were lost at Midway. An F-4F Wildcat of VF-6 is at the far right. U.S. Naval Historical Center

Lt. Col. Doolittle and Capt. Marc Mitscher, skipper of the Hornet, with the B-25 crews. U.S Naval Historical Center

Lt. Col. Doolittle with three of his pilots and Lt. Miller before the raid. From right to left, Lt. Henry Miller, USN, Lt. Col. Doolittle, Capt. Edward York, crew 8, Capt. David Jones, crew 5, and Capt. C. Ross Greening, crew 11. York and his crew landed at Vladivostok and were interned by the Soviets. After a year, they escaped to Iran and returned home.

An anti-aircraft gun crew on board Enterprise take a break during a training drill. The combined fire from ships in a task force was a daunting obstacle for aerial attackers. Lawson referred to these 1.1-inch quad mounts as "Chicago pianos," a common nickname. U.S. Naval Historical Center

Commander Henry L. Miller, commander of Air Group 6, USS Hancock, in 1944. Miller trained the Raiders how to take off from an aircraft carrier. He had a distinguished career in naval aviation and retired as a rear admiral in 1971. Courtesy Stan Cohen

Insignia on B-25 No. 11 "Hari Carrier," Capt. C. Ross Greening pilot. After hitting Yokohama, the crew bailed out over eastern China and was rescued by farmers. Greening created a series of paintings of the raid while he was a POW in Germany. Returning to the United States after the Tokyo raid, he was shot down over Italy in July 1943 and was captured. Although he escaped after two months and evaded the Germans for another six, he was recaptured and spent the rest of the war at Stalag Luft 1. He died in 1957 at 42 of a rare blood disease. U.S. Air Force Archives

B-25s on the Hornet's flight deck. Too large to stow below decks, the big Army bombers rode the entire trip lashed to the deck. The cruiser USS Nashville (CL-43) is in the background. U.S. Naval Historical Center

Another view of B-25s tied down on the flight deck. U.S. Naval Historical Center

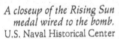

Lt. Col. Doolittle attaches the Rising Sun medal he received from the Japanese to a 500-pound bomb, which was then loaded into Ted Lawson's B-25. U.S. Naval Historical Center

A closeup of the Rising Sun medal wired to the bomb. U.S. Naval Historical Center

At 0745, lookouts spotted a Japanese picket, requiring launching the B-25s some 250 miles farther from Japan than originally planned. It was to prove a crucial variation. Now, none of the crews could plan on having enough fuel to land safely at the various strips in China. Before their craft was sunk, the picket's crew radioed warnings of the Americans' approach, but the warnings were not heeded. U.S. Naval Historical Center

A B-25 moves past the Hornet's *flight deck crew.* U.S. Air Force Archives

As Navy gun crewmen watch, a B-25 leaves the flight deck. Note the exaggerated climb angle and fully deployed flaps. U.S. Air Force Archives

This B-25 leaving Hornet is usually identified as Doolittle's. With all the bombers remaining on the aft flight deck, it would seem logical that this was the leader making the first launch. Note the camouflage pattern on the carrier's hull. At this early period, the massive shapes of larger ships were beginning to be repainted in disruptive schemes to confuse submarine crews. U.S. Air Force Archives

A B-25 circles a task force ship as the crew gets its final bearing before heading for Japan. U.S. Naval Historical Center

U.S. Naval Historical Center

Very few photos of the raid survived. Lt. (later BGen) Richard A. Knobloch, copilot of aircraft No. 13, saved these two showing the big naval base at Yokuska after he and his crew bailed out near Poyang. U.S. Naval Historical Center

A dejected Jimmy Doolittle sits by the wreck of his aircraft, contemplating what he thought was a failed mission. He couldn't know that the cheers of his countrymen, his nation's highest military award, and a brigadier general's star awaited him. U.S. Naval Historical Center

Villagers lead the crew of aircraft No. 14 through the town of Kuang Feng. Crewmen are from left to right, Lt. James Macia, Lt. Jack Sims, SSgt. Jacob Eierman, and Maj. John Hilger, pilot of the B-25, who was hurt, and is supported by a Chinese. SSgt. Eierman was also hurt during his parachute landing. After hitting Nagoya, the crew bailed out over southeast China. U.S. Air Force Archives

Ted Lawson on his return trip home through Africa. He got the haircut in Cairo and the new clothing from the British.
Mrs. Ellen R. Lawson

Lt. Robert M. Gray, pilot of aircraft No. 3, which hit Tokyo. The crew bailed out over China. Cpl. Leland D. Faktor, the flight engineer, died of injuries he suffered during his parachute landing. Gray stayed on in China to fly but was killed on August 23rd when his aircraft crashed because of suspicious circumstances. His leather jacket carries the prominent "Kicking Mule" of the 17th Bombardment Group, which provided the aircraft and crews for the Tokyo raid. In one of his first feature roles, actor Robert Mitchum played Gray in the movie of the book.
Mrs. Ellen R. Lawson

Lt. Robert Hite, one of eight raiders captured by the Japanese, is led by two guards. He was the copilot for aircraft 16 and endured 40 months of imprisonment before repatriation at war's end. Four of the POWs died at the hands of their captors: three were executed and one died of malnutrition.
Air Force Museum

Dr. Chen, Jr., and his father, April 1942. These sympathetic Chinese doctors tended to Ted Lawson, cleaning his wounds and probably stabilizing him and saving his life. The younger Chen visited the United States in 1993 and was greeted by several of the Tokyo Raiders whose lives he and his father had helped save.
Mrs. Ellen R. Lawson

Lt. Robert S. Clever (crew 7), Lt. Thomas R. "Doc" White (crew 15), Lt. Dean Davenport (crew 7), and Lt. Charles L. McClure (crew 7) pose with two Chinese.
Mrs. Ellen R. Lawson

The missionaries Alice and George Parker, who assisted the Chens, were actually Bessie and Frank England. Lawson had used fictional names to preserve the couple's anonymity from the Japanese, who killed an estimated 200,000 Chinese in retaliation for helping the raiders.
Mrs. Ellen R. Lawson

Convalescing at Walter Reed Army Hospital in Washington, D.C., Ted Lawson, with his wife Ellen, and Hal Watson (l.) greet Henry J. Morgenthau, Jr., Secretary of the Treasury, in the summer of 1942. Both raiders have recently received awards, perhaps one of several awarded by the Chinese military attaché in Washington. Mrs. Ellen R. Lawson

After returning to the United States after the raid, a smiling BGen Doolittle poses in a B-25. One of the most colorful, respected figures in American military aviation, Doolittle received his fourth star from President Ronald Reagan in 1985, long after his retirement in 1946. He died in 1993, three months before his 97th birthday. ACME

Ellen and Ted Lawson in 1943. Mrs. Ellen R. Lawson

The movie based on the Lawson-Considine book became one of the best military aviation films ever made. Quite naturally, Ted served as a consultant. Here, he is shown with the USAAF plant representative and Mr. Leland Taylor, assistant to the president of North American Aviation in the shadow of one of the B-25s used in the film. Mrs. Ellen R. Lawson

Veteran actor Spencer Tracy played Jimmy Doolittle in the film based on Lawson's book. In this scene from the movie, Tracy addresses the crew of the "Ruptured Duck" before the raid. Van Johnson, who played Lawson, is on the far right. Other Hollywood personalities include Robert Walker (second from left) and Don DeFore (fourth from left). Courtesy Fred Freeman

In this shot of the launch sequence, the overhead lights of the set are plainly visible. Van Johnson sits in the cockpit waiting for the launch officer's signal. The film's realistic flight-deck scenes and in-flight sequences represented some of the best that the 1940s and pre-computer age had to offer.
Courtesy Fred Freeman

Lawson and retired LtGen Doolittle tour the MGM Studios in 1955, accompanied by studio stars Anne Francis (c.) and Ann Blythe (r.) Mrs. Ellen R. Lawson

After leaving the service, Ted worked at North American. He wrote the flight manuals for the F-86. Here, he talks with North American Dan Darnell on the F-100 flight line in April 1957.
Mrs. Ellen R. Lawson

The Lawsons and their three children in 1957, Ann, Bob and Kit.
Mrs. Ellen R. Lawson

China. From the top of the dyke I could see a broad beach-line facing west. We had been carried across the breadth of the island.

Now as we were borne along the ridge of the dyke I blessed again the memory of Charlie, for a Chinese junk was sailing in to meet us, a few hundred yards up the beach. Our guerrillas called to the men on the junk and they called back. Here was our escape, utterly miraculous but no dream.

We left the dyke now and started diagonally toward the junk. We went along the edge of a mucky ditch that ran parallel with the beach. Suddenly, from where the junk lay, we heard a sharp, clear, "Hi-hi!"

Without a word our new coolies dumped us in the ditch. When we cried out from the shock of the fall and tried weakly to find out what was being done to us, the guerrillas who had flattened out next to us held up their fingers for silence. They peered intently over the edge of the ditch.

I raised my head so I could see a little. A Japanese gunboat was coming around a promontory off the beach. With sick, mingled fears I watched it come up briskly to the side of the junk. I could hear the Japanese questioning the men on the junk. It was torture to lie there in the ditch, waiting. Physical and mental torture. The Japanese must have spotted us, I reasoned. They must be wild to catch us, for certainly they had been informed of the raid and our route to China. They surely had found the plane by now. They would make one of the men on the junk tell. . . .

The gunboat was pulling away. We waited until it was out of sight, then the coolies picked us up again. They walked down the ditch to a point where we were parallel to and could see the tip of the junk's mast. Then they ran us quickly across the beach, slushed through the shallow water to where the junk rested and dumped us in. I rolled, groaning, into a gummy mixture of bilge water and sawdust on the floor of the junk. McClure's coolies tried to lift him in, under his arms, and he had to cry out again. The guerrillas got in with us, wary, guns cocked.

The creaking, stinking junk pulled slowly away. As it did, one of its crew rolled down lattice-work blinds to conceal us as we lay in the bottom of the boat.

Before dark we were becalmed. It was breathlessly hot. The Chinese waited patiently, then dropped the limp sail and two of them went to work with the big oar in the stern. We moved along like a snail. We groaned and began begging for water. Any water.

When it seemed as if there wasn't another breath of air to gulp in that darkening hole, it began to rain. The guerrillas understood about the water, then. They picked up bowls they found on the junk and set them out in the rain. They'd reach them in to us and we'd gulp the cool rain water and hand them back for more. It rained hard, so we got enough water.

It was crowded on the floor. My left leg was getting number all the time. Whenever I'd try to stretch it out to get some feeling in it my bare feet would jab into one of the other boys.

A little breeze came up at dark. The boatmen ran up the whining sail again and we went along through the night, desperate for medical care and trying to find comfortable positions in the muck of the flooring. McClure got braced well against the side of the junk and went off to sleep, but in his sleep he moved and his shoulders stabbed him awake.

I switched my quilt around and when I did I noticed that my left leg was bleeding a little on the ankle as well as along the thigh. I remembered scraping the ankle when I was dumped in the junk. That was the least of my worries, then.

I fell off into what I guess must have been sleep. Maybe it was; maybe it wasn't. It seemed only a few minutes before I woke up. Davenport was shaking me. I asked him what was the matter.

"You were having a nightmare."

I asked him how he knew.

"You kept hollering, 'Don't let them cut my leg off.'"

I thought that over for a while and then I asked Dav a favor. I told him that if I passed out before we got to a hospital I wanted him to see to it that no quack horsed around with my leg. He said he'd see to it.

The junk stopped about midnight. I could hear it scraping against a wharf. Two of the guerrillas pointed to their mouths and jumped up on the pier. The junk rocked for a while after they jumped. We just lay there behind our screen. When they didn't come back in an hour or two I fumbled around until I found my wet money, called one of the other guerrillas, gave him a dollar, pointed to my mouth and made a motion for him to go.

He came back in about half an hour with a big bowl of food. It was a mixture of cold rice and bean sprouts of some kind. Over the top of it were thin slices of hard-boiled egg. He also had some hard-boiled eggs in their shells, and a jug of rice wine. This was now the early morning of the 20th. We hadn't eaten for about thirty hours.

I couldn't get any of the rice and bean sprouts down. My mouth wouldn't work. But I got some of the egg slices in and swallowed them. Then I broke up a hard-boiled egg and got it down. The other boys said I should try to swallow some of the rice. They said it was pretty good. But

I was more interested in the wine. I hurt so much in so many places that I thought it might help to drink a lot of wine. But I just couldn't drink it, and neither could any of us. It was like raw, uncut alcohol. It burned my busted mouth and torn gums like lye. So the guerrillas drank it. We pulled off shore when the others returned, scraped on what must have been a sandbar, and slept.

I stood up on my two legs for the last time in my life at about dawn on the 20th. I had to take a leak. I crawled in the sawdust and bilge water and pulled myself up the sidewall of the junk. One of the guerrillas saw me. He lifted the lattice-work screen and I stood there, tottering and looking out, until I had finished. Then I lay back down.

A good wind came up at daybreak. Lifting up the blind a little and peering out, I saw we were going up a wide river. The wind held and our spirits and aches rose together. We had one moment amounting to terror when, after excited jabbering from the Chinese, two of their rifles roared overhead. But one of the guerrillas looked in on us and grinned. He made a motion like a bird flapping its wings.

We reached shakily for our cigarettes, as men do, and smoked. Somebody said, "Jesus."

In the middle of the afternoon we came up to another wharf, jutting out from the little river settlement.

The Chinese didn't get out. I thought the place might have a telephone, on which we could call Chungking. We made ringing noises to the bewildered guerrillas, held our fists to our mouths and ears and spoke. They just stared back at us.

So I asked Thatcher to go up into the village, look for a phone and put in a call. The guerrillas shrugged and the boatman shook his head as Thatcher walked up the pier. As soon as he disappeared among the milling Chinese we pulled away from the wharf. I tried to tell the Chinese that we didn't want to leave Thatcher there, but they paid no attention.

We anchored out in the river and the crew of the junk, and the guerrillas, watched the wharf. We talked it over among ourselves and decided that they were suspicious of the town; that something or somebody supposed to meet us had not appeared. Our thoughts went to the Japanese again.

Late in the afternoon there was a sudden bustle on the junk and we began to move. I called out that we wouldn't leave Thatcher, but when I got the screen up a bit I saw we were moving back toward the wharf. When we got closer I could see standard stretchers of wood and canvas on the pier. The incomprehensible machinery of Chinese aid was working again.

Getting up out of the junk and on the wharf, then

on the stretchers, was an excruciating job. It wasn't even made less painful by our expectation of impending medical care. New coolies carried us down the wharf to land, past a few ramshackle buildings and a blur of faces, and on to a wooded trail. Off this trail we'd occasionally see rather nice buildings or homes and, as each one of these came into view, one of us would say, "That must be the hospital."

But we'd always pass them. After being carried about five miles we came to a village of narrow, smelling, teeming streets. It was beginning to get dark, but the men seemed to be carrying us all the way through the village. Near the edge of the settlement, however, the stretcher bearers stopped. They carried us into the patio of a cleaner-looking little building and placed us on the ground.

There were some China Relief posters, printed in English, stuck on the surrounding walls. Pretty soon the most beautiful sound I've heard came to my ears. Someone inside was speaking English well, with a Chinese accent. An intelligent-looking Chinese with eyeglasses came out and shook hand with us.

"Anything we got is yours," he said. "We know what you have done."

I told him we needed a doctor, anesthetic, iodine, sedatives.

He looked at me forlornly, and sighed. They had nothing at this station, except bandage and a little food and water. Not even a sleeping pill, not even an aspirin tablet or any kind of antiseptic. No doctor, of course.

But we felt better after the Chinese nurses had washed us with hot water, and it was a relief to see Thatcher again. He had wandered around all that time, making telephone gestures, and finally had stumbled on to the China Relief station.

They got the belt and necktie off my leg. I had stopped bleeding and so had the others. Clever was still under the influence of shock more than the rest of us. We envied him. He wouldn't let the nurses wash all of the caked blood off his face. The nurses took off my shorts and carried away my quilt. When I was washed they gave me a pair of clean, rough, cotton shorts.

We drank more hot water, then a clear hot tea and munched or sucked on rice cakes, sweetened with brown sugar. It was dark by now, and I tried to go to sleep. But I just lay there full of pain, everything on me wanting care.

The man in charge of the station came in that night. I was glad he did. I felt so low about so many things. I told him that a lot of times, back home, I had seen people taking up collections on street corners and in movie houses for China Relief. I told him I had passed up the collection boxes more times than I had contributed and that when I'd put a dime or a quarter in the box, it used to make me feel like a pretty generous fellow. I told him I was so damned sorry I could cry. Maybe I did.

He smiled there in the dim room.

"Don't," he said. "Your money went a long way. Try to sleep; you have much ahead of you."

I lay there awake on my stretcher until after dawn. It was getting light, on the morning of the 21st, when I heard a babble of voices outside and soon a good-looking young Chinese came into our room. He introduced himself in English as Dr. C——. He looked our wounds over quickly, and what he saw was obviously more than what he expected. Before I could ask him, he told me he had brought no medical supplies with him. Nothing.

Dr. C—— and twelve coolies, carrying six sedan chairs, had walked all night from L——, he told us. L—— was twenty-six miles away. There were no roads. He told us now that his men would carry us to L——, without resting up from the ordeal of walking all night to reach this station. We were to leave immediately. The Japanese were scouring the coast line of Chekiang Province, in search of us, he said.

It was about seven o'clock on that morning when

they carried our stretchers out into the patio of the Relief Station and lifted and helped us into the chairs. One of the young nurses brought me a fresh blanket and fitted it around me in such a way as to provide a kind of upholstery for the wooden seat of the chair. She put the rest of my shredded things around me and gave me a sack of tiny Chinese oranges.

The man in charge of the station came over and shook hands. I handed him all the money I had, $13, but he smiled and handed it back to me, shaking his head. I tried to pull the wings off my shirt again, but he saw me and said he wanted nothing.

We got a touching send-off. At the near-by edge of the town, a company of Chinese troops, spic and span, stood at attention at the side of the path that led out of the primitive village. They stood stiffly, and, as we were carried by, they saluted us. It brought a lump to a fellow's throat. Those of us who could, returned the salute. I wondered if there was ever a more grisly parade.

Beyond the company of soldiers stood a detachment of Chinese Boy Scouts, dressed in the same type of Scout uniform you see in our country, only made of rougher cloth. Their faces were freshly scrubbed and shone in the early morning sun. They looked very manly when they saluted us. Beyond them stood a straight line of Girl Scouts. Behind all these were the people—silently peering over the shoulders or heads of the guard.

The path gave out after a few hours, but Dr. C——knew where he was going. The coolies walked silently across fields, up and down hills and along narrow dykes enclosing checkerboard paddies. My chair was hard, despite the padding. There were times when I thought I could not stand one more jolting bounce. When I felt I'd have to cry out and ask them to leave me behind, I'd suck on the bitter oranges and try to concentrate on the way the juice burned my mouth, the number of seeds the oranges had, and other things, so I wouldn't think about the leg and arm and hands. I couldn't pass out.

Davenport heard me moaning. "Take my chair," he called back to me. "It's built so that you can recline in it. That'd be easier on you."

But even the thought of transferring from one chair to another was pain-laden. I couldn't move. That was tough, too, because the bitter orange juice had filled my bladder until I thought it would break. I found myself envying the coolies, not only their strength but for their ability to relieve themselves. It was all so natural to them. They'd hardly hesitate; just let it go wherever they were. I couldn't. If I could only have gotten to a tree. I could have leaned against it, but it was too much to explain.

Late in the afternoon I had to change to Davenport's chair or go nuts. I relieved myself during the operation. Dav's chair was easier. I could stretch almost all the way out. And so we went on through the lifetime of that day. After dark I felt certain that we were lost, for we seemed to be doubling back, taking one tangent and then an opposite one. I'd call out to Dr. C——, and he'd come running back to me with a canteen of water. He'd tell me we weren't lost, that we were following a path or the course of paddie dykes. The night was impenetrable.

After a hell of torment, we reached L—— about ten o'clock that night. It was an indescribable eternity after we started. The village gave off an unearthly, phosphorescent glow. Dim figures moved past my chair and peered in at me. I called weakly for Dr. C—— again, and he arrived with water and a promise that we'd soon be there. It seemed that again we wandered hopelessly through conflicting streets, while I feebly raged. I felt the front end of the chair rise and for a long time we seemed to ascend very wide steps. Then the chair leveled off again and we were carried into a courtyard.

"Here they are now," I heard a British voice say.

"Thank God," a woman answered fervently.

Dr. C—— came to my chair. "My father's hospital," he said. He was utterly exhausted, I could see. I tried to reach out to touch his arm and thank him.

The voices we heard were those of Mr. and Mrs. George Parker. They were missionaries, fine people in their early forties. He was English. She was Scotch.

"You're safe here," Mr. Parker told us when we were carried inside. "You can stay here until you've recovered." Nurses began to wash us and, while they did, I asked Mr. Parker about medical supplies and care.

He looked at me soberly. "You'll get more care than anything else," he finally said. "We have an antiseptic fluid, a little chloroform and bandage. Nothing else." It was terribly hard news to take after that trip.

I had a little soup and tried to go to sleep—wondering about Ellen. I was remotely glad she couldn't see me. But the thought of her made me think of our future together. I had tried to kid myself, but I was frantic about my leg. So I tested it in the only way I could. I rolled over on it. It took a long time to do it. Then I rolled on it again. The pain crushed the breath out of me, but I felt better because I had rolled on it.

My left ankle, near the scratch I had gotten on the junk, was the size of a football when I woke up in the early morning of the 22nd. Old Dr. C——, a fine-looking elder with a long gray beard and long silk robes, came in to see us early. Young Dr. C——, none the worse for his earlier ordeal, washed out our wounds with an antiseptic that looked like weak purple ink.

While he was doing this another missionary, an Englishwoman named Mary Small, arrived and introduced herself. She represented a missionary society, was a trained nurse, rather pretty and in her late twenties. She told us she had come to L—— from Taichow, also in Chekiang Province, just ahead of the Japanese. She said it noncommittally, but a wave of helpless despair passed over me.

All that day of the 22nd I lay near a low window on the ground floor, looking at the ever-changing design of Chinese faces at the window. There was a queue beyond the range of my vision. A window-full would peer in at me and, after a while, give up their places to the next group. There were always a few children, and it seemed that almost invariably two streams of mucus would be sliding down their upper lips and then retreating back into their nostrils as they breathed and stared.

Mrs. Parker saw I was cracking up. Late in the day she came to my bed and told me she had arranged for Thatcher to move into our room and that Thatcher's roommate of the night before, a Chinese patient, would be placed somewhere else. I got a quiet, isolated room that looked out on the hospital garden through French doors.

The nurses put hot compresses on my ankle, but by the morning of the 24th the swelling had gone well up toward the knee. It was discoloring, too. I thought night and day of sedatives. The anesthesia of shock was all gone.

We had great news on the 24th. Mr. Parker came in, excited far out of his customary calm.

"We've just received word that another crew whose plane crashed is coming here," he said.

I asked him a lot of questions at once.

"I've told you just about all I know," he laughed. "Word travels fast in this country. I can never get accustomed to it. As far as I know, your friends are all right. They must be; they're walking here. One of them is a doctor. Is that possible?"

I tried to yell into the room where the other boys were that Don Smith and his crew, including Doc White, our flight surgeon, were coming in.

It was punishing, waiting for them. They straggled in late in the afternoon of the 25th. You never saw five dirtier men, but God, how good they looked! They weren't a bit banged up—just worn out. Best of all, the Japs hadn't gotten them.

They all came into my room and took a look at me.

And after a while they said things like, "You'll be okay, Lawson."

Then I got their story out of them.

They ran into the same storm that caught us, though their targets had been in Kobe. They were the last plane off and they expected a lot of trouble because they had to do their bombing about an hour or more after Tokyo had gotten it. But they found Kobe still unprepared. There was very little anti-aircraft fire, and no planes. They figured that they did most of their damage around the dock areas. They said the trains seemed to be running as usual and that the people they saw seemed in no hurry to get off the streets.

They saw the three cruisers on the way south, but didn't see the subs and mother ship. They hit some headwinds as well as that storm. Just about the time it was dark their motors began to miss. Smitty decided to set his B-25 down in the water, near an island that turned out to be just a little farther out in the China Sea than the one we crashed near. Our island, I found, was Nantien.

He kept his wheels up, of course, and dropped his flaps. They hit at about a hundred or so and skipped like a flat stone. Then the nose burrowed under and they were all under water, inside the plane. They thought they were goners. But the ship was still buoyant. It bobbed up again and floated a while on top. They were about a half mile off shore.

The ship floated long enough for them to get out the rubber raft, undo their chutes, get out through the top exits, inflate the raft and toss some emergency rations and guns in the raft.

They started to paddle away from the plane and immediately got a bad break. A wave threw them against the sharp tip of one of the plane's broken flaps and punctured the raft with a great hiss. Down went the guns and provisions, and they had to swim for shore. Doc was about the only one who saved anything. He saved two tubes of morphine, and I guess that eventually saved my life.

The boys made the beach all right, wandered around in the dark and discovered a goat pen. They started to sleep there for the night, but, after a while, the Chinese who owned the pen came out, led them to his house, woke up his wife and kids and let the crew sleep in the house. The Chinese family slept in the goat pen.

The next day the Chinese family arranged with a boatman friend—a man whose nose was eaten off by leprosy, Doc thought—and the man sailed them to our island, Nantien. There they met our very same guerrillas, including Charlie. Charlie told them about us and told them something that I didn't know. There had been a scouting force of eighty-five Japanese soldiers on our trail the day we were carried across the island. That explained Charlie's conflicting decisions at the meadow.

The same Japanese very nearly caught Smith, Doc and the boys, and would have caught them, if the boys hadn't been able to walk. The guerrillas got wind of the Japanese, rushed the boys to a Chinese temple on the island and hid them in its cellar. The boys had one gun with which to defend themselves. They stayed in their hiding place for about four hours listening to running boots and sharp voices outside. But when the trapdoor opened, and the boys backed up and Smitty aimed the gun at the opening, it was the guerrillas, not the Japanese.

Charlie, they said, sent his greetings.

Doc White had left us in the middle of the story. Now he came down from his room on the second floor of the hospital, cleaned and shaved. The boys had gone off to clean up. One of the nurses was putting hot compresses on my leg again. Doc had a pair of scissors in his hand.

"How do you feel?" he asked me, as he looked over my temperature chart.

I said I felt pretty good. He poked around my lower

leg with the blunt edge of the scissors. The leg was pulpy. Finally Doc picked a spot up near the bottom of my calf and pressed the point of the scissors harder and harder against it until it punctured the skin.

The stuff jumped out suddenly, and just kept spurting. It wasn't sickening. It was like water. Doc kneaded my leg and got a lot out. Some of the swelling went down, and I felt better.

On the 26th another missionary couple arrived. Mr. and Mrs. Fitzgerald. They were young, too, with a little girl and a baby boy about a year old. Fitzgerald was English. His wife was an American girl. She had gone to China as a nurse. Mr. Fitzgerald was one of her first patients. She nursed him over a siege of malaria and later they were married.

They were wonderful people. Mrs. Fitzgerald brightened up my room a lot with flowers. We'd often talk about the Pacific Northwest with its winter wheat and such things. I told her and the other missionaries about Ellen and the baby who was coming.

They were just plain, gentle, hard-working men and women, more completely uninterested in their own welfare and comfort than anyone I've ever known. Their days and most of their nights were devoted to us. They seemed far more interested in us as men than in us as aviators.

I was a terrible care for them. The better the other boys got, the worse I got. Clever was up on crutches, his head and face bandaged, late on the 26th. He hobbled in to visit me and to tell me I'd be up soon.

My days began to run together now. The things I'll relate consumed perhaps a week. Perhaps more.

I couldn't eat, so Dr. C——fed me intravenously. Smitty gave me a transfusion. The transfusion apparatus was a weird combination of bladder and rubbery arms that had to be kept shaking so the blood wouldn't coagulate. "It's Japanese," I heard Miss Small say, distantly. "You know, they took this village last year and set up a puppet. But they must've decided it had no value. So they stripped the town and one of the things they took was our American transfusion equipment, and left this thing."

Dr. C—— was always there with his needle. I woke up once, trying to yell that somebody had stolen all my buttons. A Japanese plane came low over the village, and I heard the thud of a bomb not far away, and later I heard the missionaries saying that it was nothing but a hand grenade that landed near the pontoon bridge leading out of L—— . . . . Staff Sergeant Williams, Smitty's bombardier, gave me the second transfusion. . . . All of Smitty's crew, except Doc, were standing at my bedside one day. They were leaving. Thatcher was going with them. Doc told me I was $1,000 richer. Chungking had sent it. "But it's a thousand bucks Chinese," he said. "That's about fifty dollars."

The little garden was beautiful when I could look out and see it. It wasn't manicured; just naturally beautiful. A stone well in the middle, magpies and hawks and buzzards often in sight. . . . Somebody outside the room talking. . . . The Japs are forty miles away and moving our way. . . . Dr. C——'s needle, until I think my veins must have cowered in my arms. . . . Flowers from the townspeople. . . . Cool water out of the spout of an enamel kettle. . . . The morbid putty color of my room's walls. . . . Sulfanilamide and sulfathiasol, from God only knows where, but bought with part of my "thousand dollars." . . . Crazy sulfa dreams almost as soon as they'd sift it in my leg and arm or pop it in my mouth. . . . The Mayor of L——, smiling and bowing to us and bringing us little gifts from the people—then going upstairs to see his son, dying of lung trouble. . . . A Chinese general pumping my hand up and down.

I remember calling for Doc and asking him to sew up the gash in the upper part of the leg. I told him I'd feel better if it weren't open. It looked so awful. . . . And the rag he put over my face, and the peace of chloroform. . . . Waking up and seeing that Doc had decided to sew only half of it, leaving the rest open to drain. . . . Purple-ink antiseptic being poured into the scissors opening in my calf and running out my ankle cuts as if down a series of pipes. . . . The boys. . . . Davenport with a cane. . . . And, yes, telling them how sorry I was about the landing.

"What the hell! It wasn't your fault." . . . Saying that I should have gone in high on instruments and bailed out.

"Aw, forget it. What's done is done. The motors would have quit no matter where we were."

I guess I looked through the wrong end of a telescope for many days. I couldn't pull myself together. You see, all this time Doc was scissoring dead flesh off my lower leg each day. He started that the night he punctured it and let the stuff drain out. Twice a day after that he'd clip flesh away, mostly around my ankle. Often I felt nothing. Doc would ask me to tell him when he touched live flesh, but he'd know, for I'd scream when he did cut living flesh. He'd give me a shot of morphine afterward, sometimes.

I asked him once about what the ankle would look like if he kept cutting off flesh. He said they'd do a good plastic surgery job on it when I got back to the States.

But it was a shock to go through with the two daily cuttings. Old Dr. C—— would stand there, holding my pulse and looking at me sorrowfully. It got to be more than I could stand, so one day I broke down and blurted that I couldn't take it twice a day.

Doc kept clipping away. "You'll either take it or you'll lose the leg," he said.

I told him for Christ's sake, take the leg. I couldn't take two cuttings a day.

Doc stopped when I said that. He gave me a pep talk, but it didn't do much good, I guess. But for the next few days he cut me only once a day. A Chinese carpenter built a platform for my leg to rest upon.

All this time the missionary women waited on me. They'd cook up different types of nice dishes, and I'd try hard to eat, but I couldn't. They would have to take them away and call for Dr. C—— and his needle. But they never seemed to regret the time and trouble they expended on me. Mrs. Parker found some brandy, once, and fixed it up in a nice egg-nog. I couldn't drink even that.

The big day came toward the end of the first week in May. I don't even know what day it was. But in the middle of that day Doc came into my room. He was very clean-looking in his uniform. But he was uncomfortable. Neither of us said anything for a little while.

I looked at him and asked him if he was going to take the leg.

"Yeah—I think so," he said.

Doc didn't ask me how I felt about it. So, after a bit, I said I wished he'd get started. All I could think of now was getting rid of that damned thing.

"That's all I wanted to know," Doc said.

The Parkers came in now. They had been waiting outside. They knew. They started talking about Ellen and the baby. They meant well, real well. I was glad the boys didn't walk in to see me then.

Dr. C—— told me about the anesthetic that would be used. It was a spinal shot. He explained that you stick an empty hypo in the lower spine and draw off the spinal fluid secreted at that point. Then shoot the same cc volume of the anesthetic into the same spot. It paralyzes everything from there down.

Chinese runners had carried the stuff to L—— from a city whose name I can't remember—days away from L——. It was just one more miracle.

Doc came back in the room. Naturally, I wanted to find out something more. I asked some questions and found that it was going to be done up on the second floor of the near-by operating building.

I said to him that I guessed it wouldn't be so bad, with it off. It would be something like wearing a shoe with a high instep.

Doc didn't answer, and for the first time I knew that he was going to take more than my foot and ankle.

I told him now, after I swallowed, that I wanted to be sure that he took it off well below the knee.

Doc was busy thinking about something else. He didn't answer, so I had to come out and asked him where he'd take it off.

"Well," Doc said, "above the knee. I'll leave you as much as I can."

It was hard to take that. Awful hard. I said I had hoped and I had thought that if it had to come off it would be below the knee. Maybe I said it over and over.

"Nope," Doc said. "If I did that, I might not get enough off. Then there would have to be another one, and your system couldn't take it."

I tried to find some answer to that, but there was nothing to say. Dr. C—— and a nurse took away the platform that was holding my leg up. That let me roll over on my side, drawing my breath in sharply, because rolling hurt a lot. And in that position Doc gave me the spinal.

I was drowsy, but I still could see all right and think and hear all right. They brought a stretcher up to the bed, rolled me on it and carried me out of the French doors and through the pretty C—— garden to that operating building. I told them to keep my head lower than my feet. I remembered that Grubb—who helped stand up for Ellen and me at the wedding—had had an operation once and had watched it being done. They kept his head up, and he had had headaches for weeks afterwards.

When we got to the operating house the men did just the opposite and started to carry me up the stairs head first. I called to Dr. C—— and he straightened it out. We came back down the few steps, turned around, and I was carried up feet first. As if it made a lot of difference.

In the operating room were Doc, Mrs. Fitzgerald, Mary Small, Dr. C——, Dr. C——'s wife and two Chinese nurses. I was rolled on the table and Doc poked around the leg a bit. It wasn't dead yet, but by the time they wrapped the lower part of it in oiled paper I told Doc I thought it was dead now.

Doc took his time. He wanted to be sure. But at last he came over to the table with a scalpel in his hand. I cocked an eye down, and he started.

I couldn't see any blood, or feel anything. But I knew he was cutting. I could see his arm moving and see him lift my leg up so he could cut underneath. He cut around once, rolled back that layer and tied the blood vessels off. Then again and tied. Then again. Then again. Four times around.

Now I felt that I could move the toes on my good right leg, and it vaguely worried me. I thought the anesthetic was wearing off. There wasn't any more of the stuff, of course. I told Doc I could move my toes.

Doc hurried. I could move my whole ankle now. I told Doc this, and the two Chinese nurses came up on either side of the table and held my wrists.

Doc stepped away and walked back quickly with a silver saw. It made a strange, faraway, soggy sound as he sawed through the bone. Except for the tugging fear that I was coming back too soon, the actual amputation was almost as impersonal to me as watching a log being sawed. I could hear the different sounds of the saw as Doc's elbow bent and straightened, bent and straightened and the teeth went through thicker and thinner sections.

Then there was an almost musical twink, and deep, deep silence inside me as Doc laid aside the saw. The Chinese nurses let go of my wrists. The nurse on the right walked around to the left side of the table. She picked up the leg by the ankle. The other nurse picked up the other, thicker end.

I watched the two nurses carry it out the door.

The sewing took some time. I was getting very nervous by now. I could move my right foot, ankle and toes about as much as I wanted to. I told Doc I could feel his sewing needle, too.

Doc would say, "Just a few more now," and I'd

watch his arm rise and dip, rise and dip. Then it would hurt again, and I'd tell him. Finally he said, "Just one more," and he kept his word.

I had had four transfusions during the week leading up to this. Now Doc gave me my fifth, and a shot of morphine that put me to sleep. Just before I passed out I saw Dr. C——, with his feeding needle.

Doc kept me full of dope for the next few days. Whatever anybody wanted to do with me was all right with me. I just lay there, back in my room. When I finally tapered off, I got around to making myself look down. Doc had sewn two rubber tubes into the stump for draining. He seemed a little concerned about the way it was draining, so he gave me some chloroform and took them out. It didn't make much difference to me. What hurt most on me were my arms. They were full of lumps and bruises from the needles. Mrs. Fitzgerald had joined the needle corps. I had no idea what she was shooting into me. All I knew is that the needles hurt, and that I couldn't sleep much because my back was now filled with bed sores.

I had a strange dream all the time. It went on whether I was asleep, drowsy or almost wide awake. It was screwy. I thought I was in a small rowboat, off the coast of China. I was rowing and making good time, but someone would always make me change into another boat. The new boat would have no oars. I'd tried to get back in my old boat, but I could never find it. I'd find a lot of rowboats but they'd have no oars.

Often I'd wake up during this dream and yet the thing was so strong in my mind that for a long time I'd still be changing boats. To try to stop the dream I'd look around the room and pronounce the names of different objects in the room as well as my mouth would permit. But the sound of my mumbling would make me drowsy again, and soon I'd continue changing boats.

The boys came in four or five days after the operation, talking about everything except the leg. They brought me a lot of stuff that people had sent to me or they had bought for me in the village. They told me about some feasts which had been thrown for them, and about the speeches they made, through translators, and how the Chinese who gave them the banquet would always apologize at great length over the quality of the food, which was always very good, they said. They had run into some good wine, too.

They sat around, smoking and talking and laughing about things, like the way bedbugs always singled out Clever.

McClure laughed, and said, "Well, Lawson, this is a hell of a lot different from hedge-hopping back in the

States," and, like a damned fool, I started to cry, and they left, uneasily.

Mr. Parker came in then. He sat near my bed and asked me if I would like him to read to me. "I have *Three Men on a Horse*," he said, "and a couple of English novels. What would you like?"

"I thought missionaries always read from the Bible," I said, in a half-joking way.

"I hadn't intended to," he replied, "but if you would like it . . ."

And so I drifted off to sleep to the sound of his pleasant voice: "He maketh me to lie down in green pastures . . . He restoreth my soul—yea, though I walk through the valley of the shadow of death . . ."

The boys had some news the next day. Mr. Parker had a short-wave radio. It was a battery set and he had a windmill generator to recharge the batteries.

He had picked up San Francisco, the boys told me. An announcer on a news broadcast was talking about the Tokyo raid. The announcer said it had been a great success. Not a plane was lost during the raid, the announcer enthused.

I told McClure I was sorry about what I had done during the earlier visit. I tried to explain that a fellow gets a funny psychology if he's had something done to him, as I had had. I said a fellow finds himself weighing everything that's said to him; weighing it against what he is and what he was, where he is and where he was. I didn't do a very good job, trying to explain. I just didn't want to be reminded of anything.

When Mr. Parker came in that day I asked him if I could hear the radio. I thought it would be nice to hear some music. Like the fine, accommodating man he was he went across the village to his house that evening and brought all that equipment to my room, fixed up an aerial and ground and hooked up the heavy storage batteries. He turned it on and got me some music from San Francisco.

It was full of static. The static was like sandpaper on my brain. I didn't want to hurt his feelings, or seem ungrateful, but finally I had to call Mr. Parker. I told him I was sorry for all the trouble I had caused him, but I just couldn't stand it. I guess I must have kept saying it, because he went out and I heard him calling Doc. Doc gave me a shot of morphine by candlelight and Dr. C—— gave me the intravenous feeding. By now it was taking five or six jabs from each of them to find the veins, or not jab all the way through them.

I started eating a little about a week after the operation. Milk at first. Dr. C—— had one of those stunted cows that give about a pint a day. They boiled the milk for me, corked it in bottles and lowered it in the well outside my room to cool it. Soon I could take strained soup and then I began eating almost everything. I went to town on mush, different kinds of preserves, gray bread I could chew with my remaining back teeth and ground-up greens, something like spinach.

One day Mrs. Fitzgerald said, "What do you want to eat? Anything you want." So I said I'd make it tough for her. I told her I wanted Swiss steak, and I tried to laugh because I knew it was impossible. That night for dinner I had Swiss steak. It was water buffalo. Mrs. Fitzgerald was a wonderful woman.

The hospital cook, Wong, was a great character. He had been cook at the Shanghai Y.M.C.A. before the Japs came in. The missionaries told me that he had three wives, but he'd never admit it. He came into my room occasionally to chat, and I'd confront him with his polygamy. Wong would stand up, sort of offended-looking, place his hands on his heart and say, "No, no, Lieutenant. No three wife—*two* wife."

I thought Mrs. Fitzgerald had reached her peak as a food magician when she conjured up the Swiss steak. But the very next night she and Mrs. Parker came in with a roast pheasant. Mrs. Parker's Chinese neighbor had winged it illegally in town. Maybe that's what made it taste so good.

I was so thin when I began eating again that I

could see both bones in my right leg and my kneecap looked like a turret on the rest of my leg. I figured I weighed about a hundred pounds, or eighty less than when I took off for the raid. I was filling out now, however, until I couldn't see my ribs.

I heard from Charlie. By some means known only to him he sent me his calling card, of all things, with a tiny head picture of himself stuck in one corner. That wasn't all. He sent word that the Japs had grabbed some of those islanders who helped us get away and had tortured them.

There was something vaguely alarming about the visits of the Mayor and the General to the hospital those days near the middle of May. They would take Mrs. Fitzgerald or Mr. Parker or Doc aside and talk to them very earnestly for long periods. Then Davenport walked in one day, with his cane.

"How do you feel?" he asked me, casually.

I said okay. What else can you say when you know you're going to hurt for weeks or months?

"How long do you think you'll be before you get up?"

I said I couldn't tell, and asked him how soon Mc-Clure and Clever and himself expected to be in good shape.

"We're just about all set now," Dav said.

That left only me. So I asked him if there was any great hurry.

"Well—no," he said. "The other boys are just getting kind of anxious."

The next day Mr. and Mrs. Fitzgerald, Doc and Dr. C—— came in with a large wrapped package. Their good nature was a little forced.

"We've got a present for you," one of them said. They unwrapped it and, of course, it was the crutches. A local carpenter had made them.

Dr. C—— also told me that one of the local families wanted to make some slippers for all the boys, so he measured my foot. I kept looking at the crutches. I used to ski a lot.

Doc seemed very eager for me to get used to the crutches. I finally gave them a trial about May 15th. It took me fifteen minutes to sit up and sidle to the edge of the bed, I was so weak. After a dizzy spell passed, I stood up on my right leg and went slowly across the room to the French doors. I got out on the little porch outside and flopped into a chair. I sat there a while, looking at the garden, and by the time I got back to the bed I was so exhausted I slept for an hour or two.

The Chinese who made us the slippers—they were black silk—called the next day. He bowed low and handed me my pair. Then it struck him all of a sudden.

The poor fellow got very flustered and backed out, painfully embarrassed. I felt bum a while, but it passed.

It wasn't important. Nobody around the hospital was mentioning the really important thing: the Japs were forty miles away. Maybe less, by now.

On Sunday, May 17th, the Parkers came in early and said they were giving a party at their house late that afternoon. They wanted me to come. I told them I didn't think I could make it. But they said that I could, and must. They tried to make it sound very gala. They would send a chair for me.

I wanted to go less than ever when I saw my face in a mirror, just after that. I had decided to get some of the beard off. I was a discouraging sight. My mouth had bled into the beard and matted it. There were lice, too.

In the early afternoon two coolies came up to my window with a nicely padded chair. I got into it after a struggle, and they carried me down the hill of steps to the village. McClure, Davenport and Clever also were in chairs, and we went through the streets like a procession. L—— was an interesting place—full of strong smells, colorful markets and streets so narrow you could almost touch the facing building fronts.

The Parkers' house was on the other edge of the town, about three miles from the hospital. We recognized it by the windmill that generated power to recharge the radio batteries. It was a pleasant, clean place with a nice yard. They carried me into the yard. The coolies lifted me out of the sedan chair and put me down on a kind of kitchen chair near by. Then they lifted me up with the chair by the lower rungs and carried me into Mr. Parker's library.

Mr. Parker was waiting for me. He asked me if I had written to my people. I told him I hadn't; that I thought about it a lot, but that I couldn't bring myself to write. I asked Mr. Parker if he'd write to my mother. I told him how sick she was, and I explained that it would be better for him to write; he'd know the best approach. He said he'd do it immediately and did— but the letter, I heard, was held up at Chungking along with other letters from the men to their families.

"Now, how about your wife?" Mr. Parker asked me.

I told him I didn't want him to write to Ellen. I had some more thinking to do about that.

I was carried out on the porch that commanded a view of the city and we had tea. Swank. Mrs. Parker had made an angel-food cake with the egg whites of all the extra eggs that had been given to us at the hospital by the people of L——.

Mr. and Mrs. Fitzgerald arrived and so did an elderly missionary couple who had been in L—— for twenty-two years. The old man was having trouble with his eyeglasses, he told us, but he had had a set of test lenses which opticians use to find the type of glasses you need. Doc matched up the different lenses for him and got a combination that worked—so that the old man could write in to some larger city and have new glasses made.

The old missionary showed me pictures of his two boys, one of them in the British Navy. I asked him why the boys didn't go into missionary work, too, and whether he was disappointed.

"No," he said. "Everyone has his call in life. It is better to answer your true call."

It made me think a little of my research ambition.

At dark I was carried back into the house, for dinner, and noticed a lot of packing cases in the English-style living room. The Parkers didn't seem to want to talk about them, so I let it go.

We had a great dinner: roast duck, bamboo shoots, peanut butter and canned butter. The water was almost cold. It had been in the well for a couple of days.

They had to talk about the Japs, eventually. They were guarded at first, but I told them not to worry about me. I knew. I asked them what they were going to do.

The Fitzgeralds were going to S—— with us the next day—which was the first news I had that we were leaving and where we were going. I got them to repeat the name of the village. The Parkers explained the packing cases, then. They were sending some of their stuff to S—— to keep it from falling into the hands of the Japs.

I asked what about the Parkers themselves.

"Our work is here," Mr. Parker said. "We'll stay as long as we can."

After dinner something very interesting happened. The Chinese Boy Scouts had had what they call an Olympic meet that afternoon. One school had sent its Scouts from a distance of thirty miles. They had walked all night and arrived in L—— this Sunday morning. During the day they had run and jumped through the track meet, then gotten back into uniform to join the other Scouts who were paying us a visit.

It was all very formal and impressive. Our bunch stood in the Parkers' living room, near the packing cases, and the Scouts marched in, saluted, and left gifts for us. The Girl Scouts followed them, and they too saluted and left little things for us. They let me sit throughout the ceremony.

We started back to the hospital at nine o'clock that Sunday night in a driving rain. I shook hands with the Parkers before I left. Some sudden ache of departure filled me. I tried to tell them how grateful I was for everything they had done for me. But it's hard to put things like that in words. I told them I'd see them the next morning.

It was still raining on Monday morning, May 18th. Our chairs were assembled and Doc was stewing, eager to get going. We had heard that coolies were reluctant to carry during a rain, but they did this day. There were hurried good-byes to our friends. My spare clothes, presents and crutches were strapped to the chair. Doc had dressed my stump and the boys had found a pair of trousers for me, which Doc pinned up to fit. It was draining and bleeding.

Before we left the grounds of the little hospital, Dr. C—— came to my chair, smiling blandly. "I want to show you something," he said, and ordered my coolies to carry me around to the other side of the hospital. They set me down beside a coffin. It was a new one, made by the same Chinese carpenter who had made my crutches.

It was to have been mine.

The Parkers and the old missionary couple saw us off. They ran along beside our chairs in the pouring rain, patching the leaks in the little roofs with oiled paper. What can you say to people like that?

The last I saw of them they were standing in the rain, waving good-bye and saying we'd meet again soon. And saying they'd follow along the trail after us as soon as they settled a few things at their missions.

They waited too long.

We made quite a party, Mr. and Mrs. Fitzgerald, their children, their No. 1 boy and young Dr. C—— were with Doc, McClure, Davenport, Clever and myself. Dr. C—— had decided to go on to Chungking to offer his services to the Chinese Army as a doctor. He asked us if we would recommend him to our "important friends" and seemed humbly grateful when we told him that of course we would. I asked him about his young wife. He said that when the Japanese came she could go to her people in the hills.

It was just a month since the Tokyo raid.

We crossed the pontoon bridge which the Japanese plane had bombed and entered a trackless, wildly beautiful land. There were paths now and then, sometimes none. We went along all that day. Clever's coolies spilled him out of his chair, but none of his bandaged cuts reopened when he hit the ground. I kept my fingers crossed.

Late that night we got to S——. We were carried into a kind of patio of what must have been a tea house, then McClure and I went to the Fitzgeralds' house. Doc came there and re-dressed my leg.

We had dinner, and then, while Mrs. Fitzgerald was looking out for the children, Mr. Fitzgerald sat down to talk to us.

"I'm worried," he said. "Not about myself. If they come in on us in a hurry, I could get to the woods and hide out. But I can't very well take Mrs. Fitzgerald and the children.

"The servant problem is peculiar," he went on. "When there is a threat of a Japanese attack, the servants demand more money and they keep raising their demands as the Japanese get closer, until they won't work for love nor money. Mrs. Fitzgerald and the children need them very much."

McClure and I suggested that he send his wife and the children along with us when we left in the morning.

Mr. Fitzgerald thought it over for a while, then made up his mind. "No, I think not," he said. "We'll take a chance on getting out on time. The Japs have never been in here. I don't think the village has any military value, even though it's on a river. I guess we'll get along all right. See you in Chungking, maybe."

It was tough that night, trying to sleep. When I finally did doze off I was promptly awakened by the sound of a gong in the street and the voice of a Chinese calling out something I couldn't understand.

Mrs. Fitzgerald came in early the next morning with a breakfast of English muffins and tea.

"Did the noise wake you up last night?" Mrs. Fitzgerald asked, cheerfully.

I said it did and asked what it was.

She laughed. "Oh, it was just our town crier. He was telling the people to leave the village because the Japanese are getting closer."

I said I hoped she'd leave with the children, and with us.

"Heavens, no! When you've lived here as long as we have, you realize that there is always time. The Chinese give you plenty of warning."

They stayed behind when we took off that morning for the village of W——. "See you in Chungking," Mrs. Fitzgerald said, as she tucked us in. I sensed with a rotten, empty feeling that this would be the last time I'd ever see them. It was.

Now it seemed to me that I could feel the very breath of the Japanese on my neck. Three Chinese soldiers appeared from nowhere, as we were carried out of the village, and marched at the side of our chairs. They sniffed the air of the thickets and wooden paths for Japanese patrols. The coolies who carried us must have been fully aware of the danger, too. They jogged along at what must have been a faster than normal clip, but under the circumstances it seemed excruciatingly slow. It made a fellow want to keep looking back.

The coolies carrying the other fellows made a game of this urgency. McClure's carriers shuffled past us on a narrow path and each of them bumped the old man who was carrying the front of my chair. And giggled when he staggered and nearly fell. Clever's carriers slapped at the old man as they went by. Soon we had fallen a half mile, then a good mile behind the others.

There was a sturdy young coolie carrying the rear poles of my chair. He kept calling up to the old man in front to hurry. I could feel the young one straining and pushing against the poles. He wasn't any more anxious to get away from S—— than I was.

The old man up front, with a face and stooped shoulders as old as China itself, was rapidly failing. Twice he was violently sick on the dirt of the path. The second time, the Chinese soldier, who had remained by my chair when the others went on, kicked the old man as he lay there vomiting. The old man got up and carried me a little farther, while the boy on the back end strained and urged him along.

Finally the old man fell once again and just lay there, panting. The Chinese soldier stood over him for an instant, looking down. Then he cocked his rifle and pressed the muzzle against the back of the old man's head. I couldn't believe it. It seemed like an age before I could make my mashed mouth yell something.

The soldier stopped and looked around at me, apparently unable to understand why I should be interested. The old man looked at me, too. I didn't know what to do then. I couldn't say anything to them, so I took out the silver watch somebody had given me in L——a queer key winder—and waved it back and forth on its chain and beckoned to the old man.

He got up and came forward with his hand out, pitiably. But I was afraid that if I gave it to him then he might just run off with it. If he did that the soldier would kill him, and I'd be stuck there on the trail far behind the others. So when he reached for the watch I made a negative motion with my head, pulled back the watch and pointed up the path. I was trying to make him understand that I'd give it to him when we reached our destination.

I guess it was a cruel thing to do, but I just had to get away. He didn't understand. I took out a piece of scrap paper, burned a couple of matches and tried to make a quick sketch of a coolie, running. The impatient soldier walked away during the middle of all this, but the coolie finally understood. He picked up his burden and we started ahead very slowly.

I worried along for an hour or so, feeling so damned helpless, but then the soldier reappeared with a fresh, younger coolie. The soldier slapped the old man and the poor old guy slunk off across a field with his head down, like a beaten animal. I called to him but he never turned. He never got paid.

Doc White had to stay in my room at W—— all that night. He didn't have to tell me that my stump had become infected.

The Japs might be close, but we couldn't resist that breakfast the Chinese fixed for us early the next morning. We started off with partly hard-boiled doves' eggs dipped in peanut oil and rolled in brown sugar.

"Rocky Mountain oysters!" Davenport said as he bit into the first of the ten each of us was served. And Dr. C——, of all people, laughed.

After that came boiled chicken and boiled chicken eggs, some sort of poached chicken eggs with a strange sauce over them and boiled water. That was the morning McClure finally gave up on chopsticks. He rummaged through his stuff until he found a silver fork which the silversmith at L—— had pounded out for us.

We started out for the village of N——, which sits on the top of a neighboring mountain. It was the cruellest kind of climbing. To the fear of capture was now added the fear that one of the coolies would slip on a mountain path and we'd all plunge to the rocks below. But we made it by two o'clock on that afternoon, May 20th.

The other boys didn't get in until an hour later. Their coolies had purposely stalled in the hope that the boys would get out of their chairs and walk. They finally made the coolies hurry by refusing to give them cigarette butts until they did hurry. The coolies arrived, smoking furiously.

We started down the mountain after hurriedly stuffing a strange mixture of food in our mouths—a Chinese actually had Nabiscos for us—and for interminable hours we were carried through wild but freshly verdant countryside.

It is a bad feeling to expect a burst of Japanese gunfire at every turn of a path, every clump of trees. Our winded coolies did the best they could, but it was maddeningly slow.

Late that evening, to the relief of all of us, we caught an unmistakable whiff of human excrement. We had all learned by now that this supposedly lowest of all earthly aromas was a signal of approaching safety. You see, in the rural Chinese districts, each village places three or four barrels under a shed on the outskirts of the town. The barrels are partly sunken into holes in the ground and, of course, are used as public relief places. When they are filled to the brim, the Chinese uproot them, put them aside, and install empty barrels in their places. When twenty or so barrels have thus been collected the contents are carried away for use as fertilizer in rice paddies.

You become aware of the barrels at a distance of two or three miles sometimes. They became the suffocating, yet ever welcome, milestones of our escape, for each meant a village and each village was putting us closer to Choo Chow Lishui—and a plane.

A mile or so before we reached this heady but most welcome village, an emissary of the village came out on the trail to welcome us. He was a bright, nervous-looking Chinese with glasses. He spoke good English. He shook hands a number of times.

"I know all about you, Lieutenant," he said to me. "Corporal Thatcher came through here about a month ago. He told me everything. The other boys were with him." He meant Smitty's crew.

I asked him how they were. "Fine," he beamed. "We beat them."

I asked him to say that again.

He grinned. "We beat them. Our church basketball team challenged them and beat them by two points. A wonderful game!"

We leaned back in our chairs. "Good Christ," Davenport said softly.

They carried us into another patio at this stop and then to a nice room upstairs in the building. There was a bowl of preserved kumquats and other sweets on a table in the room. That night, with complete disregard for the Japanese spring drive southward, the local dignitaries feasted us with chicken and pork fixed three or four different ways, several varieties of fish and a good light wine.

Early the next morning we went on. There was a hint of a wider trail and the Chinese provided us with rickshas. But Doc decided that one of these would be too bumpy for me. The leg might bleed even more profusely. So I went on in the sedan chair, and, as it turned out, I had less trouble than the others. They all broke down on the rough path on the way to our next village.

We didn't have much chance to forget the Japs. About noon that day, while ascending the steep hill that lay between us and our destination, a Zero came straight at us over the ridge. I guess he was going too fast to notice us or do anything about it. He streaked out of sight.

We got to the village in the early afternoon, hours ahead of our next means of travel. We sat there, waiting and worrying until dusk. Then the always magic-working Chinese produced a 1941 Ford station wagon and a Chinese charcoal-burning truck. God knows how.

Doc thought it would be better for me to ride in the truck because I had to stretch out. Three quilts were put on the floor of the truck. At dark I was placed on top of them and off we went. The others, except Dr. C——, went in the station wagon. Dr. C—— sat in the dark truck with me.

I had looked forward to this for a long, long time, but after a bit I began to pine for the sedan chair and even Charlie's stretchers. The springs of that truck just weren't springs. Every time we'd hit a bump, and we must have hit a million, I'd leave the floor. The next bump would get me coming down. I used both my hands to keep what was left of my leg from banging. That didn't help much. It just thumped and bled and throbbed. We kept going.

I can still hear Dr. C—— trying to comfort me. "Ah, Mista Lawrson. All right?" he'd ask in the darkness. I could only moan.

Behind us now I heard one explosion after another, regularly paced. When I could speak, I asked Dr. C—— what they were.

"Ah, Mista Lawrson," he said, sad and placid.

"Japanese too close. So Chinese blow up road behind us, just after we pass. . . . I didn't want to tell you."

Late that night we stopped and, when they carried me out of the truck, I guess I was pretty well broken down. But I did hear them say that we had reached Choo Chow Lishui, the place where I had wanted to land the Ruptured Duck. As bad off as I was, and as speechless with relief as I was at the thought of reaching the end of our long journey, I still noticed how the men around us were pronouncing Lishui. We had said it something like "Lishooey," to Charlie, that night in the fisherman's hut. They were saying it "Leesh-way." No wonder Charlie didn't understand us.

All of us now called for Dr. C—— to ask him to find out about the relief plane we were sure was here. He went away and spoke for some time with the Chinese officials. Then he came back and told us that there would be no plane here. The Chinese had been forced to blow up the airport to keep the Jap planes from landing there.

I guess I must have passed out after hearing that, for I don't remember what happened for two or three hours. The next thing I remember was that I was in bed. It was dark and someone was shaking me awake. Whoever it was said it was 3 A.M. and that we had to get out of Choo Chow Lishui. The Japanese were bringing mechanized stuff over the very roads the Chinese had blown up earlier that night.

Doc dressed my stump hurriedly, throwing away the soggy bandage, and I was carried outside to a small bus, camphor-burning, and stretched out on the back seat. We got off a little after four, cold and hungry and hopeful that the bus would keep going.

That was a ride! We soon nicknamed the Chinese driver Johnny Beep-beep. The bus's brakes were only third in importance in his mind. The horn was first and the steering wheel second. He was the damnedest driver I ever saw. Nothing bothered him, including our yells.

We were getting out of Chekiang Province now, and Dr. C—— was having trouble with the changing dialects. About one o'clock on that afternoon of the 22nd we raced like wrath through a town on whose gate was posted a sign showing a skull, crossbones and a rat. Dr. C—— thought it might be notice of bubonic plague in the place. But on the outskirts of the village we decided that we'd just have to eat, for we had had nothing that day. So we stopped and were relieved to find that the sign was simply a poster advertising a kind of "Kill the Rat Week" in that village.

About an hour after lunch, Johnny Beep-beep brought the careening bus to a grinding stop on a yawn-

ing curve in the mountainous road. We had just passed
a little settlement of eight or ten houses. We looked out.
There was nothing in sight except a limitless view of
rolling countryside, green with spring.

Johnny turned and said something to Dr. C——.
Dr. C—— said "Ginwah?" incredulously. We knew that
meant air-raid.

"But there isn't anything in sight," someone said.
"Let's go on."

"No, it is better to do what the driver tells us," Dr.
C—— said. We sat there about twenty minutes. It was so
quiet and it seemed such a waste of time that I asked
Dr. C—— to find out how Johnny knew there was an
air-raid. He spoke to the driver.

"He saw a warning signal in the settlement we just
went through," he said.

An hour later we were ready to doubt that, and said
so. Dr. C—— transmitted this to Johnny. Johnny spoke
without passion. Dr. C—— translated.

"He said that he knows, from experience, that the
Japanese planes will shoot any moving thing on a road.
It is better to wait, he says."

The boys got out to stretch and look down the deep
hill to the valley below. What they saw made them excited. I hobbled out of the bus and looked over the
edge. A little river meandered through the valley. On it,

in countless flatboats, were hundreds of Chinese families, their possessions banked around them, poling down the river in obvious flight.

We bounced on to P—— late that afternoon but couldn't find the place where we were supposed to go. We drove aimlessly through the crowded streets until nearly dark, wondering if we were just stupid or whether something had gone wrong. Then the boys spotted an elderly white woman, the only one we had seen for days. She was dressed in severe black. Davenport got out of the bus and spoke to her and found that she was the missionary we were looking for. She led us to the mission, and the officials of the town caught up with us there.

The Chinese contempt for Japan's spring offensive was a nerve-jarring but stirring thing to see in action. P—— was going about its usual routine, but you never got the impression that it was an ostrich. Everybody seemed to know the Japs were coming that way. There was no hysteria and very little emotion. The officials of P—— insisted on giving us a feast that night. When they heard that it was Clever's birthday, their joy was touching and genuine. They even found ripe peaches for him.

I couldn't stay long, and, after I was in bed, I asked myself out loud why it was that every bed I slept in had the same overpowering smell. It must be some sort of national disinfectant the Chinese use, I said to myself. After a while I couldn't stop saying it. Doc came in and gave me more morphine. Then I could say the truth. It was my leg, not disinfectant. I had been trying to kid myself.

It was still dark when we got up on the morning of the 23rd. Johnny Beep-beep was in his driver's seat, beep-beeping for us. We started off and got to a bridge. The middle portion of it was so narrow that it didn't seem possible that we could make it. The boys got out and walked across. Johnny got out, too. He squinted across the bridge like a man aiming a rifle. Then we backed up, got a running start, and made it. We scraped on both sides and probably bulged it a little. But we made it.

You drive on the left side of the road over there. At least you're supposed to. But somebody forgot to tell Johnny about the rule. He'd go around a curve with a deep drop on our left and a precipice rising off the road on our right, and he'd scrape the precipice all the way around the bend. Of course he couldn't see what was coming the other way. That didn't worry Johnny.

I looked up once and there, coming right at us, was a big camouflaged Chinese Army truck with foliage tied on the top of it. The road was very narrow. Johnny's brother must have been at the wheel of the Army truck. When Johnny gave him a beep-beep, he got back a beep-beep. I shut my eyes and waited for the crash, but Johnny had gauged it just right. The camouflaged truck scraped all along our side and moved us over two or three inches on the road. Johnny didn't bat an eye or change his thirty-miles-an-hour speed.

The blown-up airport at Choo Chow Lishui was a shock, for we had counted so much on getting to a plane in four days after leaving L——. But when we got to Nanching about 2 A.M. on the morning of the 24th, after more than twenty-two hours in the bus, it was even tougher to learn at Chinese Army headquarters that the field there also had been destroyed. We had talked of little else for two days except getting the plane there. Now it would have to be Kian.

There was iodine at the Nanching headquarters, the first we had seen since the crash, five weeks earlier. All of us were welted and sore with bedbugs and lice. I still had the bed sores on my back. Doc dabbed all of us from head to foot.

I slept late the next day, which was Sunday. For some reason beyond our understanding, we weren't going to travel that day. The Chinese Army had decided we'd better not. There wasn't anything to read or do—except wonder about Ellen—so I got up and practiced with my crutches around the headquarters. I wished I had already written to Ellen.

Davenport rushed in late in the morning, bursting with news. He had met up with the two Irish Catholic missionaries of Nanching and had walked down to their place. They had a radio. They got a San Francisco news broadcast for Dav. The fellow on the radio had said that Doolittle was back in the States, that he had been made a General and had gotten the Congressional Medal of Honor. And that everybody else on the flight was going to get either the DSC or the DFC. Davenport couldn't make out which. Anyway, it was exciting. Not only that but the Catholic missionaries were going to come up to see us later that day and tell us their story about Hal Watson, our buddy, who had come through Nanching a month before, injured.

Just after noon, a Chinese Colonel called on me in my room and brought along his phonograph and an armful of records. I told him to shoot the works and play them all, as I shifted myself into a more or less comfortable position in bed. He looked pleased as he cranked up the spring and put on a record.

Then out of the horn came a thin, reedy kind of chop-sticky song. It had never occurred to me that they'd be Chinese records. The Chinese musical scale has five notes, but there seems to be some ban against using more than three of them. After a couple of records that sounded exactly alike, I looked helplessly across the room at Dr. C——. Dr. C—— was sitting there in a chair, a little dreamy-eyed, his head moving back and forth, keeping time with the three scraping notes.

The Colonel played his records for about two hours. I smiled at him after each one, but finally after one of the records I asked him if he had an American record.

"Certainly," he said. "The best."

He reached down to the bottom of his pile and drew out a thin platter and put the needle on it. It had a distant, scratchy melody. Now and then you could hear a woman singing in a high-pitched voice. Then the record would run into worn-out spaces and only the needle noise was heard. When it was over I asked the Colonel what it was.

He looked at me, surprised. "Jeanette MacDonald, of course," he said. Then he played the rest of the Chinese records. He went out of the room once and the thing ran down, but by this time the kitchen help and other servants were standing in the doorway, listening. When the spring would run down one of them would leap into the room and wind it up tight again—and the records played on.

The Catholic missionaries came late in the afternoon, with cigarettes and the story about Watson.

Watson's arm was badly dislocated when he came through Nanching. The missionaries didn't know how it happened, except that it had happened in a parachute jump. They had tried to set the arm for Watson, but there was no anesthetic. So they gave Hal a few drinks of whisky and, when he was feeling pretty good, one of the missionaries asked him if he'd mind changing chairs. Watson walked across the room and started to sit down in the new chair. As he did, the missionary grabbed him under the bad arm and pulled up on it as Watson dropped his weight. The missionary hoped to snap it back in place. But the pain was so great, even through the sedative of alcohol, that Watson fainted. Watson went on the next day, still in great pain.

The mosquitoes were as hungry as the bedbugs that night, and bigger and smarter. They even went after Dr. C—— and got inside the netting around his bed. He reached out and lighted the candle near his bed and brought it inside the netting to try to smoke or burn them out. But the only thing he did was set the netting on fire.

Dr. C—— started to curse in Chinese while he swatted out the spreading flames.

I started to laugh and couldn't stop. It must have

been weakness or something, but I couldn't stop laughing.

After a while Dr. C—— came over to my bed. "Ah, Mista Lawrson," he said, regretfully. "You wake?"

We began to roll the next day. There was a 1942 Ford station wagon waiting for us when we got up. Doc decided that it would be better for me to ride in it, sitting up, than to go on in the bus. The road was good and our time was better. We got off at 6 A.M., had lunch at 9:30 at Lingtse, where Dr. C—— bought a beautiful vase as a gift for Ellen, and headed for Kian and the plane for Chungking, safety, and medical care.

A charcoal-engined ferry boat broke down with us that day and we drifted crazily down a stream until another ferry came after us, hooked on and stopped us until ours could be fixed. But we still made Kian at 6 o'clock that evening and put up at an AVG hostel. There was no plane. The field was gone. We were numb with disappointment—but one would surely be at Heng-yang.

The Flying Tigers had gone on from Kian, but there was an AVG radio man there. And not only American food, but showerbaths. Two intelligent Chinese took care of our needs at the place. One was T. M. Wang, general secretary of the Officers Moral Endeavor Association. The other was Koo S-ken, interpreter for the AVG. He knew more American slang words than I did.

We sat around talking for a long time to Koo S-ken and smoking his cigarettes. He told how the Japs seemed to single out the universities and schools when they bombed Shanghai. I said that seemed like a waste of bombs.

But Koo S-ken said, "No, those Japanese are smart guys. They know that education produces leaders. So they attempted to crush the source—our universities and schools."

I gave him Ellen's gun that night. It was rusty by now, but he seemed to appreciate it very much.

The next day I tried the crutches a little for more practice, but didn't do too well. We had an air-raid warning when a Jap observation plane flew over the city, but that was the extent of that. Dr. C—— bought Ellen a fine Chinese tea set and Koo S-ken, who had heard about Ellen, gave me one of those Chinese silver buttons—symbols you see on the dress hats of Chinese kids. He told me it would bring Ellen and the baby good luck. Late the same day a Chinese Colonel and his wife and daughter visited us, after we had our first haircuts. They all knew Doolittle. He had come through Kian and they had entertained him.

On the morning of the 27th a number of high-ranking Chinese officers called on us and left their cards. The Mayor of Kian arrived at 6:30 A.M. that morning to present us with embroidered shirts and new shorts.

We got off about seven o'clock, had lunch at Ning-hang and, when we stopped later in the day at a place named Cha Ling, with tire trouble, we were joined by a somber Chinese soldier. As we started off with him in the station wagon, he handed us Luger automatics. Dr. C— spoke to him for a long time, and then listened while the Chinese spoke for five or ten minutes. Finally the soldier stopped.

"Bandits," Dr. C— explained.

But we saw no bandits and pulled into Heng-yang at 9:30 that night. The Chinese soldier dutifully collected all our guns and left us.

The plane couldn't meet us at Heng-yang. The field was barricaded against Jap planes and thus ours.

There were pictures of Doolittle, Gray, Watson and Holstrom at Heng-yang—all bearded and dirty and strange-looking. I looked at them while Doc dressed my leg and wondered what had happened to them and the others.

We were in Heng-yang most of the next day. We learned that when Thatcher and Smitty's crew came through they got some excitement. The Japs bombed the city all three days they were there, and they watched the whole thing from a pagoda on a neighboring hill. The morning they left the city they had hardly gone before the Japs were back. This time they must have known something, for they bombed and machine-gunned the pagoda. It made me more thankful than ever that even in our helpless condition our loyal Chinese had spirited us this far along in our journey. There was never a thought of betrayal.

That afternoon of the 28th we drove through the streets of Heng-yang on a sightseeing and shopping tour, looking at the holes where buildings once had been. There were a lot of stores in the city, and wide streets. The boys left me in the car, to make better time when they shopped. It was interesting, watching the people. Every beggar and every tradesman had a different kind of noise-maker or a different-sounding cry to identify the thing he was selling or the urgency of his want. The people came by the station wagon in endless streams. There were always faces pressed against the window, staring at my stump and broken mouth. And, a greater curiosity, my white face.

We were joined on the shopping tour by a Heng-yang merchant, who presented me with an embroidered scroll which I treasure very much. It was his concept of the American eagle. His people had sewn and stitched all night on it. He also presented all of us with sword canes.

The train came to Heng-yang. We got aboard late in the afternoon, in an English-type compartment. We crawled and jerked through the night to Kweilin. This was our new great destination. This is where the plane would certainly be.

There was an ambulance at the station for me, but it was one of those camphor buggies, and I said to hell with it. I had had enough of their springs. I rode to the AVG hostel in a station wagon.

The hostel at Kweilin was set in a woods away from the town and a mile or two from the airport. And there we had a great treat. I think I could smell that coffee a good two miles away. It was too good to be true; but there it was. I don't know how much we drank. Just then the Japs didn't seem important. We had coffee and an intact air field.

The hostel was new and spotless. The Flying Tigers were elsewhere once again, but the radio man was there. The place had a nice lawn in front of it, and separate rooms for all of us.

The plane wasn't in, but that would have been too much to expect, even of the Chinese. The AVG man said he had been in radio contact with Chungking and that the plane would be there the next day. To corroborate that, a Chinese Colonel, who had known Doolittle for years, came to visit us that afternoon and told us he had been informed that the plane would arrive.

The wrong kind of plane came the next day. Twelve Japanese bombers drummed over in close formation and bombed the city and airport.

Their coming was no surprise. In their bewilderingly casual way the Chinese have an amazing system of air-raid alarms. We were having breakfast when the first warning was sounded. It was a strange sort of "siren." The noise was made by a Chinese hitting an old automobile brake drum with a spike. As soon as we found out what it meant we started to get up from the table.

"Keep your seats," the AVG man said, continuing his breakfast. "The planes have just taken off."

We asked him how he knew.

"I can tell by the way the fellow's beating the brake drum," he said, pretty bored about the whole thing. "You'll know when the planes get closer. He'll start beating faster and faster." And he went back to his food while we picked at ours and listened to the brake drum.

He was a nonchalant fellow, that AVG man. He had come up to Kweilin just before the Japs had broken through General Stilwell's line and over-run the country. He had gotten out with an American jeep, a

Tommy gun, a ton truck filled with gas, ammunition and food. He had a boy drive this for him while he drove the jeep—and in the jeep next to him he brought out a very beautiful Anglo-Burmese girl.

The man was beating the brake drum a little faster now; then much faster. We looked at the AVG man lingering over his coffee and I guess all of us thought of what had happened to the pagoda just after Smitty and the boys had left. Finally the AVG man got up and stretched. We jumped up and followed him to a nearby cave that was the hostel's shelter. The planes were over the city and the field a few minutes later, giving both of them hell.

That same day we had a nerve-racking disappointment. After the Japs left we heard another plane coming. We got outside and saw a Chinese National Airways DC-3—our plane—go over our heads and aim for the AVG field. Some of the boys got into the jeep and rushed out to the field. But the plane had gone. We just couldn't believe it. We had counted on being in a hospital that night. The thought of standing any more pain was too much for all of us. But the plane had simply gone. We found out later that it was never intended for us.

The next day was Sunday. We had another alarm but saw no planes. In fact, that evening the boys went down to the village in the jeep to a movie. It was *Union Pacific* with Chinese sub-titles. I couldn't make it. Dr. C—— must have felt sorry for me, for he brought in an armload of firecrackers and some punk he had purchased in the town.

"We'll have nice fun and shoot firecrackers, Mista Lawrson," he said.

So we sat on the porch and lighted the little fuses and flicked them out on the lawn. A group of Chinese gathered around and seemed to enjoy the noise. That was just too much for me—after the bombing they had undergone the day before. I went back inside and found some reading matter. There were several copies of *Collier's*, a *Reader's Digest*, *Time* and *London Illustrated News*—all about a year old.

The plane didn't come the next day, either. That was June 1st. Nor the next, which was very stormy. McClure and the AVG man went down to the field in the jeep, in the rain, and radioed Chungking again to ask about the plane.

They came back with some news. The ship had been forced back once by the condition of the field and once by the storm.

But the plane finally came. It came the afternoon of June 3rd. We heard it coming first, then saw it—a DC-3 with our Air Corps markings—and we yelled and waved from the hostel. The only transportation we had to the field was already down there. The field was two miles away, over rough land.

We just had to wait. I can't describe it.

Some terribly long time after that—maybe half an hour—we heard the jeep coming. And then saw it. The AVG man was driving it. With him were Captain Tex Carleton, a classmate of mine at Kelly, Ed McElroy, who was on the raid, and Davey Jones—with a medical kit.

I knew I'd start crying as soon as I heard Davey's voice, and damned if I didn't.

You see, Dave was the first one of the boys I had heard from, at L——. The never explainable Chinese grapevine brought him word, after he reached Choo Chow Lishui, that Doc was going to take my leg. Davey sent me a letter by a series of runners. I couldn't read it when it arrived, so Mrs. Fitzgerald did. It had a few cuss words in it that made her blush as she read them. But it meant a lot to me. Davey never mentioned the leg in the letter, but I knew he knew.

"We've got a lot of unfinished business back at home," he reminded me in the letter. His wife had just had a baby. Mrs. Holstrom was having one.

All of us were nuts to know what had happened to the others. Davey and McElroy had the dope. We sat around the hostel, and they began talking. They talked most of the night. Some of the following we learned later, but most of it we heard from Davey and McElroy that night in Kweilin.

Doolittle ran into a few Japanese planes as he went in, but his B-25 had too much speed for them. He hit Tokyo at exactly the time when a propaganda broadcast, in English, was telling whoever was listening in that Tokyo could never be bombed.

Doolittle flew so low over a baseball park that he broke up the game. He got his bombs and incendiary away on factories and warehouses. On the way out he went fast across a field full of red and silver training planes and, according to his navigator, Lieutenant Henry Potter, you could hear Doolittle cussing without the aid of the inter-phone because he had nothing else to drop.

He went in high over the China coast, and over the storm, judging his time and distance. At about ten o'clock that night of April 18th he decided he was as close to Choo Chow Lishui as he could get. He ordered his boys to bail out and then he jumped into that pitch-black rainy night.

He landed in a rice paddy that had been freshly fertilized with human excrement, and freshly ploughed.

He waded through it to the nearest dyke, took off his shoes and threw them back in. Then he curled up on the dyke and went to sleep, using his parachute as a cover.

The next morning he decided he'd need the shoes for walking. So he waded back into the paddy and rescued them. They were resting nicely on top of the stuff. Then he started walking. He reached a village very soon, got his bearings and discovered that if he had chosen to walk off at a slightly different angle he would have fallen into the hands of the Japanese, whose patrols occupied positions quite close by. He later found his smashed plane.

York, who was our Operations Officer at Eglin, landed in Russia. He got down near Vladivostok, the only one of the sixteen planes to get down whole. The Russians interned him and his crew. York wasn't scheduled to go on the Japan raid. He was assigned at Eglin with the understanding that his job would end when we got to the coast. But he begged the CO of the 17th Group so hard that the CO finally okayed him the rest of the way.

McElroy told us that he had very little trouble. He didn't get much anti-aircraft, got away, flew in high over China, couldn't find the field and ordered his boys to bail out. McElroy had time to crawl back to the tail of his ship, after putting on the automatic pilot, for a smaller satchel from the contents of his B-4 bag. He put in emergency rations, extra shirts, shorts and his shaving equipment. Then jumped out—kind of fashionably—with his bag packed.

Everybody else in McElroy's crew landed safely, got together after a few villages and went on to Chungking. And back to work.

Davey said he saw one of his bombs hit a power plant in Tokyo. He said the building suddenly looked like a barrel, with the sides rounded out and the top circular. Then the "barrel" blew up.

Hoover, who took off just behind Doolittle, reached China when it was still light. He got under the storm, swung down a series of valleys, and just before dark set his plane down in a big rice paddy. He had to keep his wheels up, of course. The ship skidded in on its belly, chewing up the props and flaps but not a man was hurt.

He had a tough time destroying the plane, which was a part of our plan. Unless we got to a friendly Chinese field we were to scuttle the ships, to keep them from falling in the hands of Japanese. With that in mind, all of the planes carried a large incendiary cylinder.

Hoover got out his incendiary, put it on a gas tank

and started it burning. But something went wrong and the fire went out. The boys then got out their axes and tried to hack through to the wing tanks, but they couldn't get through. So Hoover uncocked a gas line near one of the engines. A stream of 100 octane ran out on the ground. He tossed a match into the pool on the ground and got away from there as fast as he could.

The plane was soon a crackling bonfire. Curious Chinese came from all around to watch the strange spectacle. They crowded very closely around the plane, but fled when the ship began spouting like a Roman candle.

Watson, who weighs over 200 pounds, bailed out about midnight and came down through heavy rain and intense darkness. As he got closer to the ground he pulled out his flashlight, pressed the button and pointed it toward the ground. He wanted to be set, physically, for the landing. But the beam didn't reach that far.

Then he had a sudden fear that the chute wasn't open, or something might have gone wrong with it, for it was smaller than a man of his weight should use. So he flashed the light straight up and he could see the big white canopy over his head.

But that wasn't all he saw. His right arm was sticking straight up in the air, twisted in the chute cords. In the excitement, he had not felt it get snarled and wrenched upward when the chute opened. He pulled his arm down and stuck the thumb of that hand between his teeth, to hold it down.

Watson landed on his back in the shallow stream. He couldn't move his arm. He couldn't get to his feet. He couldn't roll over on his bad shoulder, for it had begun to pain very badly now, and he couldn't roll over the other way because the flow of the stream he was lying in had bellied out the chute and was pulling in the direction away from the good arm. He tried to unbuckle his chute harness, but that's a two-handed job.

With his good left arm he reached into his shirt and took out a tube of morphine. He broke the seal but smashed the needle, too. He got out another tube and jabbed the point through his wet shirt and into his shoulder. The pain of his arm was now unbearable. He wanted to pass out, and did.

He slept in the creek until the next afternoon, cut away, got out of his chute harness and began walking. He found a Chinese shack within a few hundred yards and went in, shaking from head to foot with a chill. The Chinese put him in a bed, covered him and lighted pots of charcoal under the bed.

Watson couldn't make them understand who he was or where he wanted to go, but the next day he saw what turned out to be a paper maker walk past the hut with a basket of his wares. He bade his kind but wholly bewildered hosts a quick farewell—after giving the wife the chute—and set out after the paper maker. The man led him to a town.

Watson had plenty of excitement over Tokyo. The anti-aircraft fire was heavy. He kept looking out at the wings, waiting for holes to show in them. He got a bomb in on a tank plant among other things, but on the way the same three cruisers we had all seen opened fire on him. He was flying very low. One of the shells struck the water near by, close enough to spray water over the plane. Sergeant Scott, Watson's tough old gunner who has been an army flyer for twelve years, fought off a pursuit plane that came after them when they were at bombing level, and, when the cruiser went to work on them, Scott wheeled his machine guns around, fought back with what, in that case, amounted to a cap pistol. But he gave that big cruiser a battle its crew will remember.

Sergeant Scott is one hell of a man. He described the scene over Tokyo as "A nice, sunshiny day with overcast anti-aircraft fire." When it came time for him to bail out over China, Scott took along a pint of whisky and a pack of cigarettes. Watson ordered him and the others to get out at 10,000 feet. We had been told that we couldn't trust the reported heights of some of the hills and mountains over which we might have to fly.

Anyway, Scott came down through the pitch-black rainy night for what seemed like a long time, and then he felt himself break through the light branches, twigs and leaves of the upper part of a tree.

Then he stopped, swung like a pendulum for a while and slowed down. He knew his chute was caught in a tree, but he couldn't see the trunk of the tree. There were no branches in sight and he couldn't see the ground. So he struck a match and dropped it, but it sputtered out. Then he lighted a cigarette, got a good red ash on it and let it drop.

He watched that red ash go down and down until it was little more than a pinpoint of light. He reached up and gave the chute cords a tentative tug. They seemed to be holding all right. So he said, "To hell with it," drank the whisky and went to sleep, dangling there.

When he woke up at dawn he saw where he was. The tree that had caught him was ten feet away from the rim of a precipice. The ground was about a hundred feet below him. Scott began fanning his arms and twisting his body. That started him swinging. Finally he got close enough to the trunk of the tree to hug it, get loose from his chute, climb down the trunk on the side away from the drop and get away.

Charlie Ozuk, one of the navigators, wasn't as lucky as Scott. When Ozuk landed he scraped down the rough face of a cliff. The chute hooked on the top and flung him against the face of the drop. The blow cut his shin very badly.

Ozuk hung there, bleeding all that night and all the next day. On the morning of the following day he had enough strength to pull himself to the top, where he passed out from exhaustion. He regained consciousness late in the afternoon and was just crawling away on hands and knees when the Chinese found him. Ozuk's shin became infected.

Hilger led the raid on Nagoya. He put his bombs on an aircraft factory, an oil storage warehouse and a military arsenal, and strewed his incendiary all over a military barracks. He didn't see a plane in the air, and the anti-aircraft fire was wild.

Hilger's rear gunner, Staff Sergeant Ed Bain, said a funny thing. One of the anti-aircraft puffs appeared about a hundred yards away, the closest of many aimed at them.

"Hey," the gunner said into the inter-phone, "they're *shootin'* at us!" as if it wasn't allowed.

When the time came that night of the raid for Hilger to bail out, he tried to get up from his seat to start for the well, but his chute wouldn't fit through the narrow opening between his seat and the co-pilot's. Hilger unfastened one side of his chute so he could slip past. The gas was going in a hurry. Hilger dropped down through the well without remembering that he had unfastened one side of his harness.

He got a terrific jolt when the chute opened. It hurt his back and thigh. He tore down two trees and was knocked cold in the landing. The Chinese nearly shot him as a Jap.

Bob Gray, the tough "bridesmaid" of our wedding, ordered his men to bail out with what he thought was plenty of room. But he was much lower than he realized. Bob's chute swung him only twice before he hit the mountainous ground over which most of the boys bailed out. It knocked him out. When he came to he ached all over. After moving around awhile he felt better, walked up a long hill and spent a cold night under his chute.

Gray's gunner, Corporal L. D. Faktor, was killed. When Bob gave the bail-out order on the inter-phone, Faktor called back, "I can't hear you. What did you say?" Gray called back, "Get out of there." Then, fearing something had gone wrong with the inter-phone, Gray sent one of the crew crawling back to the gunner's place. There was a chute exit there. The fellow came back and told Gray that Faktor had his chute on and his hatch open. To make sure, Gray called back there once more. There was no answer. He assumed Faktor had gone out. That's when Bob jumped.

The Chinese found poor Faktor next to the wreck of Gray's plane. His chute bag was sprung but little of the chute had come out. Shorty Manch, Gray's co-pilot, identified him in a Chinese village by what was left of the kicking-mule insignia on his leather jacket.

Manch was probably the most heavily armed chutist who ever jumped. He went out with two .45's, a .44 calibre rifle which his folks in Virginia sent him just before we left the States, a .22 automatic, a Luger, extra clips of ammunition, a hunting knife, a Bowie knife and axe.

We used to kid Shorty a lot about that rifle, and once he yelled back at us, "Don't kid *me*, suckers. I'll make my last stand with this shootin' iron. 'Manch's Last Stand' they'll always call it." He was sure proud of it.

Before he jumped that night of April 18th, Shorty saw to it that every weapon was in its proper place on him. He was well weighted down, but he couldn't bear the thought of going out without some Baby Ruths. He stuffed a lot of them in his shirt, open at the collar, and dropped down into the night.

His chute opened with a loud report and jerked him so badly that it shucked the Baby Ruths right out of their wrappers and out of his shirt. Shorty just molted candy in mid-air. But, worst of all, for Shorty, his grip was broken on his rifle and three of his four pistols.

Shorty's six-foot-seven body frightened an entire village out of its huts. But he convinced them that he was friendly by holding his nose and making a face in front of a Jap flag.

Holstrom probably had the most comfortable chute landing. He came down in a big bush that tangled his chute and harness so badly that he couldn't get free. He struggled for a while, but it was so dark he couldn't see a thing, much less start working on the snarled cords.

So he pulled the chute up over him and went to sleep. When dawn came he was very glad that he hadn't fought too much the night before, trying to get loose. The bush that held him sat on the very edge of a fifty-foot drop on to rock.

Greening, who designed the cheap bomb sight, had the toughest time over Tokyo, but got in some great licks. Four new-type Japanese pursuit planes came up fast behind them as we approached the city. Greening hugged the ground so close that he flew under some power lines in the hope that the pursuing planes would hit the lines.

But the Japs missed the wires and came after him.

Greening's boys had to fight. They shot down two of the planes and the others wheeled off, and by that time they were coming up to their targets.

Greening got rid of his block-busters from 1,500 feet, but his own incendiary almost got him. His bombardier's aim was too good. He let the thing go as Greening dived. It fanned out over a gasoline refinery and must have hit three or four storage tanks simultaneously. They went up with a terrific explosion and Greening, Ken Reddy and the other boys in the plane were thrown around inside from the shock of the explosion below and behind them. A little closer, and it would have knocked the plane to pieces.

Greening decided that when he jumped out over China that night he was going to tour the countryside with enough to eat. When the gas was about to give out, he got back in the navigator's place, picked up two armfuls of canned goods and short rations and asked the boys to pile a few more things on top of his load before they jumped out. The boys did.

Then Greening jumped, embracing his big load of provisions. He was going down through the night at about 180, congratulating himself on how thoughtful he was to prepare himself for perhaps many days of wandering on the ground, when suddenly he snapped out of his reverie.

"Good Godamighty!" he said. "I haven't pulled the ripcord!"

This called for a little more thought. He tried to figure out some way to pull the cord yet save the food. Then he decided that if he pulled the cord in a great hurry the cans and packages would continue falling at the same rate he was falling—then he could reach out and hug them to him again.

That's what he tried to do. But as soon as he let go of them the wind caught them and they flew all over the place, though Greening pulled that cord in what must have been record time. He said later that it was just like having a big grocery-store shelf fall over on him.

Technical Sergeant Waldo Bither's chute opened in the plane and Lieutenant Thadd Blanton had a terrible time repacking it before the engines began sputtering.

Howard Sessler had a lot of trouble on the ground before he found a haven. The village into which he trudged, a day after bailing out, provided him with a bus, and he started off in style. But the bus was attacked by Zeros. Sessler and the driver jumped out and threw themselves in a ditch. The Zeros swung around and strafed them as they lay on the ground, but the bullets missed.

Sessler got out of that scrape, then contracted malarial fever. So did Jim Parker, Watson's co-pilot.

The Japanese captured two of our crews. Later, when they bragged about it over the air and said they had convicted our fellows of "inhuman acts," they mentioned only four men. They mentioned Bill Farrow, Dean Hallmark, Sergeant Harold Spatz and Corporal Jacob Deshazer. The Japs said at first that, these men would be put to death if Japan were bombed again.

Farrow and Hallmark were the pilots of the two planes. Since we started out with five men in each plane, that left six men unaccounted for by the Japs. The Chinese grapevine insisted that two men in each plane had been killed, but their names were unknown. Four of the six men unaccounted for by the Japs were Lieutenants Bob Hite, Bob Meder, Frank Kappeler and Chase Nielson. The Chinese had word that Nielson had been bayoneted, but there was no way of checking on that.

Wendell Furnas, an American who came back on the *Gripsholm*, after sharing a Japanese cell with J. B. Powell, the newspaperman the Japanese crippled, told us some months later that while in jail he had spoken to or seen eight of our boys, imprisoned in the same place. Furnas was removed to another jail the day after the boys were brought in, but he knew Nielson was in the next cell. He thought one's name was Farrell. That had to be Farrow, for he described him perfectly. He said there was a little fellow who didn't say much whose name sounded like Deeter. That was Corporal Bill Dieter. Another one he knew as either Peter or Meder, which, of course, was Bob Meder. He was sure there were eight, which leaves only two missing. We had to assume that, like Faktor, they had paid the toughest price.

Farrow, who changed co-pilots the day before the raid, had horrible luck. He got through the bombing, made his getaway, reached China, and then had the terrible break of landing near a village controlled by a Japanese puppet government.

The loyal Chinese of the village immediately got in touch with Chungking. The Chinese Government attempted to bribe the puppet and get Farrow and the boys. But the puppet finally turned them over to the Japanese. The puppet was assassinated shortly thereafter, the Chinese said.

The same thing may have happened to Hallmark. The Japs said on the radio that Hallmark's men had been captured "and were being returned to Japan."

We lost every plane, if York's plane in Russia is counted. Eleven of our original 80 men were captured or killed. But, with the exception of York, Bob Emmons, Nolan Herndon and the other boys who landed in the plane near Vladivostok, fifteen of the sixteen planes and seventy-five of the eighty men reached China. Just as the original communique said, not one plane was shot down during the raid itself. I think that was a terrific feat, and a tribute to the planning behind the whole, vast, complicated engagement.

At first the Japs said we had hit nothing of a military nature. We expected that kind of lie. They said their air-raid warnings spread 800 miles along the Japanese archipelago, and that ten planes took part in the raid. Of these, they said, nine were shot down either by anti-aircraft fire or pursuit planes. People continued with their luncheons undisturbed, the propaganda broadcast said, and only two theaters cancelled their Saturday matinees in Tokyo—where the air-raid alarm lasted eight hours.

They guessed that we had come off three carriers, "spotted at a distant point off the eastern coast of Japan proper," and, after stating that Japan could expect such attacks "as long as the United States has carriers," added that steps would be taken to punish those spreading "baseless rumors." Tokyo said forty-eight hours after the raid that fires were then under control. Then denied there had been any fires.

They boasted that they knew about the raid in advance and had bombed Chinese airports "in the Lishui section of southeast Chekiang Province." They admitted loss of life amounting to "about 4,000," and three planes. Chungking said on the radio at the same time that the planes had not come from China. Washington broadcasts said it was our answer to Pearl Harbor and Bataan and "the beginning of a great offensive." The President, as you know, named Shangri-la as our take-off field. I thought that was a good gag when the boys told it to me that night we sat around the AVG hostel in Kweilin.

"You think it was worth while?" one of the boys asked me before we went to sleep that early morning of June 4th.

I thought it over for a while, trying to see the whole thing objectively. When I finally said that I did, I meant it. We'll probably never know just how much damage we caused. The important thing, I figured, was that our people got a lift out of it. It made them sure that we could go to work on the Japs, no matter how far away they were.

I hadn't thought much about our people, before that night. A fellow doesn't volunteer for something like the Japan raid, bomb the place, try to get away and, in my case, lose a leg and say, "This is for the dear people." You just don't say or openly feel those things. You think about yourself most of the time; whether you'll have guts enough to go through with the thing, and whether you'll get away with it. It's only later, when you add up things and get the sum, that you think of the people. And the cause. And then you hope you've done both of them some good.

We took off from Kweilin's little airport at five o'clock on the morning of June 4th, and when we were in the air a little more than an hour the AVG man we left behind radioed us that the Japs were bombing the field.

That was the closest call of all—and the end of a month's fear of capture.

We reached Kunming by 9:30 A.M. and got a nice reception. Some Flying Tigers were there with their sharknosed P-40's. Great guys with plenty of dough. Two of them—Hasty and Olsen—had been classmates of mine at Kelly and Randolph. We had a nice reunion by the side of the DC-3 while Doc was dressing my stump and waiting for an ambulance. They told me how they paired up to fight the Japanese planes, and how some Jap fliers either didn't take parachutes up with them or refused to use them. They had seen many of them just jump out of the attacked planes. They also showed me what I thought was a string of P-40's on one edge of the field. They were papier-maché, the boys told me. The Chinese had made them for the Tigers, and the Japs wasted a lot of bombs and bullets on them.

After Doc had finished with me I went up to the near-by hostel and found that Hasty had sent me a bottle of good Scotch. Davey, Carleton, McElroy and Dr. C—— stayed at the field. When Davey came into my room an hour or so later I asked him where Dr. C—— was. I had a drink for Dr. C——.

"He got orders at the field to proceed right to Chungking," Davey said.

I never saw or heard from Dr. C—— again. I never got to say good-bye, never had a chance to thank him. He was the most loyal man I ever met. There wasn't anything he wouldn't or didn't do for us during those weeks at L—— and on the road. He waited on us night and day, never complaining. He never got or wanted a penny.

Later on, in a letter to the War Department, after it asked us to supply a list of Chinese who had helped us, I tried hard to express my gratitude and respect for Dr. C——. But when I wrote the letter there were no right words to put down.

At Kweilin it was decided that we wouldn't go on to Chungking. McClure and I, at Doc's recommendation, were to be flown to Walter Reed Hospital, in Washington, D.C., for treatment, after a checkup at New Delhi. McClure's shoulders were still giving him a lot of trouble. They had set wrongly. Doc didn't have to tell me that I needed a further amputation.

I was in enough pain now to welcome passing out from lack of oxygen when we climbed the 19,000 to clear a hump of the Himalayas the next day, June 5th. We came down at one of our big new bases in India.

Bob Gray was there. After the raid, he had been assigned to transport work, along with Dick Joyce, another raid pilot who had come through great. They were given three P-40's to use when the Japs would come over to bomb their transports. They weren't getting much rest.

That day I saw Gray for the last time. We flew on to another huge new field, refueled, with the temperature at 128, and had our first ice water. It felt like a blessing in my mouth. Before dark on the same June 5th we came down in New Delhi, and put up at Hotel Imperial. I found out that we'd go on soon, without treatment there.

The hotel was almost unbearably civilized. It hurt to look at the mounds of fine food, the frilly curtains, the deep rugs and furniture, after all our privations. I slept in a huge bedroom with two of General Stilwell's medical officers. They had just walked out of Burma with the General. They had malaria and dysentery and were treating each other.

I was thinking a lot about my family now, as we went into the home-stretch. So, on the next morning, June 6th, I went down the street on the crutches to a place named the Ivory Palace. I had been paid in Kunming—and found that we had gotten only a buck a day subsistence from the time we left the coast until we took off, instead of the $6 we figured on. It's a regulation, but we had forgotten, and on the *Hornet* had played poker against the Navy as if we were rich. But I still wanted to buy some little things to take home.

I had trouble getting around in the shop, but I finally got up to a counter and noticed uneasily that a helmeted Colonial was staring at me. I guess I looked like a bum.

"Seen a bit of the war, old boy?" he asked, not very interested. He stared at my hump and pushed-in face.

I was sensitive about things then. I wanted to rap him over his pith hat, but I realized that I might as well begin getting accustomed to parrying unfeeling questions. So I told him a canary had kicked me, and bought Ellen an ivory letter opener.

Back at the hotel I tried to write her a cable, but couldn't. I just didn't know how to tell her.

One of the things I often thought about during the tough days at L—— was ice cream and apple pie. Kid stuff, but it preyed on my mind so much that I swore that if I ever got out to a big city I'd eat myself glassy-eyed on apple pie à la mode. So that afternoon in New Delhi McClure and I went looking for it. And we found the best possible way to the best place. We spotted a couple of American soldiers who looked as if they knew their way around, and they led us straight to the place. There wasn't any apple pie, but what a job we did on ice cream!

I couldn't sleep again that night. About midnight I went downstairs, hired a carriage and rode around for the rest of the night. About 3 A.M. I saw the two soldiers walking down the blacked-out street with a girl, and invited them to ride with me. We rode around New Delhi, singing a few songs we knew.

We took off at 9 A.M. on Sunday, June 7th, from New Delhi and flew to our last stop in India, Karachi, and saw the Stratoliner which was going to take us the rest of the way home. Greening, Hilger, Smith, Holstrom, Wilder and a few others were there. Some of them had been ferrying fighting ships to several fronts, for this field is a kind of clearing station for such traffic.

We were going home together. We were a mob by this time.

At eleven o'clock that night they carried me into the Stratoliner, and we flew all night to a field near Baghdad, where the British had a breakfast of fish and eggs for us. We took off right after it, flew over the Holy Land and the Suez Canal to Cairo—and got there a little after noon.

The boys were invited to make a trip to the Pyramids and Sphinx, but I couldn't go on account of the walking it entailed. But I went downstairs with them, and, when they had gone, I went into the cable office, to try it again.

I picked up a pencil in the cable office, wrote out Ellen's name and address, then just looked at it for a time and crumpled it.

You see, I had talked to some of the boys about Ellen, especially to Hilger, Greening and Jones—for the wives of Hilger and Greening were with Ellen. I asked them for advice. I told them I had been thinking about this for a long time and that it was making me very nervous. But I couldn't bring myself to tell her. I told them I didn't know how to put the words down so that they wouldn't hurt Ellen or the baby. Yet I figured that no matter how I told her or when I told her, it would be hard for her to accept.

One of them suggested that maybe their wives could tell Ellen, but I asked them please not even to tell their wives. I told them I had a plan that I had thought of suddenly: I'd just stay in Walter Reed Hospital until I had all the work done on my leg and face and learned to use the artificial leg. Ellen could think that I was still in China or India. Then, when I was right, I could walk up to her and tell her all the things that had happened.

We were just about to take off from Cairo on June 10th when Clever, who had come through the hell of all those face wounds, and Ozuk, who had hung over a cliff, bleeding for nearly two days, were both stricken with appendicitis. They were ready to get in the plane. Doc sent them back to a Cairo hospital.

We got to a base on the Nile in the middle of that afternoon, had a chance to shop a little and had dinner that night in the officers' mess. Later, one of the boys let out a surprised sound as he thumbed through a magazine. A June 1st copy of *Life* had been flown in and left there. It had all our pictures.

"Golly, somebody does care," one of the fellows said.

I looked at my picture and then at myself in a mirror. Different fellows.

We took off late that night and flew until morning

to a Nigerian field, flying high over a camel caravan carrying five-gallon tins of gas to some new American outpost.

I was all mixed up inside. I wanted to get home, but I didn't know what I was going to do when I got there. I wished I had written Ellen from China, but when I looked at myself—the leg was abscessed now—I was glad I didn't. My mouth was healing all out of shape. Of course I had no teeth.

Jack Sims, Howard Sessler and Griffith Williams, bombardiers on the raid, were at Nigeria. We buffaloed with them awhile, then flew on to one of the fields we've built on the Gold Coast.

We stayed there until the 13th, having the Stratoliner's engines checked for the flight across to South America. The people there were very good to us. They took us on a "bush" trip, a picnic lunch near old Fredericksburg Castle, and it gave us a chance to take some snapshots of wild-haired natives and their goona-goona wives and daughters.

On the 13th, late, we flew on to a West Africa field, had dinner and took off that night for the trip across.

When everybody was asleep that night on the Stratoliner, I made my way up the aisle on the crutches and stood behind Niswander, the big plane's pilot. The copilot, Kratovil, was away from his seat. Niswander motioned to it, and, after a little trouble, I got into the seat and leaned back, looking at the stars in the black sky.

He was a nice guy, that Niswander. He could read my thoughts, I guess, for I was just thinking how much I wanted to feel the ship's controls in my hands when he said, "I know how you feel. Take it for a while." He took it off the automatic pilot.

I flew the Stratoliner for an hour. It helped. I had been curious to see if flying bothered me mentally.

There is a three-hour time change coming over from Africa, so it was still only a little after midnight when we flew into Natal. We refueled and flew the rest of the night to Belem and spent June 14th there. We walked around the streets near the Grande Hotel, to shop and to give me more practice, and had a drink at an outdoor café where the music was great. I wished Ellen could have heard some of those sambas. She can really dance.

Trinidad, our stop in the mid-morning of June 15th, looked like the most wonderful place on the trip home to all of us. It had not only Coca Cola but slot machines, just as ornery as the ones in the States. On the same afternoon we flew to Puerto Rico.

I had to begin to think now about getting a little slicked up. I picked up a shirt and some trousers at the post exchange, bought some new wings and dug out the silver Lieutenant's bars the Chinese had hammered out for me. I decided to keep wearing the black silk slipper I had worn from the day the embarrassed Chinese had given me a pair.

The room assigned to me that night at the Puerto Rico field was upstairs in the barracks, and by the time I started to go up the blackout was on. It's a real blackout there. I wasn't supposed to switch on a light, but getting upstairs in the dark was more than I could manage. I tried flashing on a hall light, to get a quick look at the steps, and then flashing it off. But the moment it would come on I'd hear yells to turn it off. I would wait awhile, then try it again. And the yells would come as soon as it went on. It must have looked as if I were sending flash signals to somebody.

Finally a tough Sergeant came out and started to curse at me. Then he turned the light on. He helped me upstairs. It was the first time I had tried that and it's tough to do, at the start.

Somebody was in my bed upstairs. They had changed my room to the ground floor without telling me. It took even longer to get back downstairs and, when I finally got to my room, I couldn't sleep. I went outside and talked to the guards until it was time to leave.

In the morning light we flew over the Florida Keys

to a field near Palm Beach. Hilger and I had breakfast there: two quarts of milk, two chocolate milk shakes, bacon and eggs and a stack of hamburgers. It may sound disgusting now, but it tasted awful good that day.

We talked about Ellen and I told him that my plan was best. I told him that my only fear was that somebody else might tell her. I wanted to be the one to tell her, but not until the right time.

I thought Ellen was still at Myrtle Beach with the other wives. We were scheduled to fly over the beach, so we asked Niswander to buzz them on the way north that day. He made three big circles over the little settlement and went on. I didn't know then that Ellen had gone back to Los Angeles to be near her people and my mother, but the other wives saw the plane.

We reached Bolling Field on the afternoon of June 16th—the end of a trip nearly all the way around the world by plane, ship, stretcher, flat-boat, junk, stretcher again, sedan chair, truck, bus, station wagon, train and plane again.

Niswander had radioed ahead for a Walter Reed ambulance. McClure and I waited for it at the plane, and finally it came.

You think of some funny things, irrelevant things, when your life is suddenly filled with the unreality of being badly hurt. On the way to the hospital my main thought, aside from the feeling of relief that Ellen hadn't been tipped off, was the wonderful springs of the ambulance. Whoever designed them did a great job. I guess in the back of my head I was trying to find some usefulness for myself, and my mind was going back instinctively to the thing I always wanted to be.

At Walter Reed we were taken up to Ward Five and into Watson's room. His arm was still in a heavy cast. They had operated on him when he arrived a week before, to get the shoulder back in place, and he was coming alone fine. We ate dinner off trays in Watson's room that evening, and bulled. A nice nurse brought McClure and me another full tray after we finished the first one. Colonel Peterson of the Medical Corps came in and roared laughing at the way we ate.

While we were still eating, Doolittle came in. He didn't have to go to that trouble. He had to leave his office and his work, but it shows you what kind of guy he is. He said he was sorry he wasn't at Bolling Field when the plane came in—he hadn't been told—and that he'd see to it that we got the best possible care. He's kind of like a father, I guess.

I tried to stand up when he came in, but he put his hands on my shoulders and wouldn't let me. I don't think he knew for sure that my leg was off until Doc told him at the War Department.

We talked awhile about the raid and the trip home, then he asked me if there was anything bothering me. I said that if I could get a good night's sleep I believe I could think better.

"How about the family situation?"

I said I'd like a good night's sleep before I did anything about that.

"Do you know about your mother?" Doolittle asked.

I was afraid to ask him what about her.

"She's had a stroke. She's pretty bad off. I'm sorry."

I didn't say anything.

"What do you want to do about your wife?"

Doolittle knew the baby was coming. So I told him that I wanted to stay at Walter Reed until I was all right, and I asked him if he could fix it so Ellen would think I was still abroad.

"That would be a good idea, except that I've already written your wife and told her you were injured and on the way back," Doolittle said, "but that I didn't know the extent of your injuries. That's all I told her. You'd better do something about it."

The doctors gave me two nembutal tablets that night and knocked me out for seven hours. That was the longest I had slept at one time since sleeping off the spinal anesthetic after the amputation.

Doolittle called Ellen in Los Angeles the next morning. He told her where I was and that I was safe. When he came out to the hospital to see us later that day I asked him if he had told her about the leg.

"No, I didn't," he said. "I told her that there was something else I couldn't talk about over the phone, and that I'd airmail her a letter."

The following day, the 18th, I got my first letter from Ellen in a long time. She wrote it as soon as Doolittle hung up, I guess.

"You'll never know how relieved I am to know you're back," Ellen wrote in one part of the letter. "I'm coming to Washington just as soon as I can. At least I can see you every day.

"They wouldn't tell me what happened to you, yet, but I can't imagine your being sick very long. . . . There isn't much to tell about your Mom just now. After she had the stroke on May 21st [that was the day I finally got to Choo Chow Lishui, I thought to myself] she lost her speech. She is gradually gaining it back, but it will take a long time. I'll tell her I'm going to Washington to be with you, but it would be better right now if she didn't know where you were in Washington. . . . I'd love to talk to you on the phone, but since I am going to see you I'll try and wait. I can start practicing my patience now on you, and then I'll make a better mommie."

Ellen must have sat down at her desk as soon as she finished reading Doolittle's letter about the leg. She was great about it in her air-mail letter to me. She didn't make a point of it.

She told me about her trip home the month before, and something about the car. And the clippings she had been saving. Ellen said I'd better write or wire my mother, but just tell her I was back and okay. Ellen didn't think my mother was well enough to hear about me, for the time being.

It wasn't until near the end of the letter that Ellen got away from what she was trying to do: make me know that our world was going on just about as always. And even then the way she put it was so right.

"I'm glad to know the truth. My imagination has been running away with me," Ellen wrote. "Darling, it could be so much worse. I've had so many nightmarish dreams that you didn't come back at all, and others in which you completely lost your memory and refused to believe I was your wife. Those were horrible.

"There is no reason in the world why we can't lead a perfectly normal life and do the things we've planned.

"When I do see you I'll do my best to control my tears. But, should there be any, please don't misinterpret them. Because they'll be tears of happiness and joy."

I went down the end of the hospital corridor to the phone booth and put in a call for her. Her father answered the phone and called her in from the yard, and soon I heard her voice on the phone.

I don't know what I said at first. It was about her letter, and how much it meant. Then I asked her not to come. I told her the trip might be too much for her, for she'd have to go back across the country to have the baby near her people. We didn't know anybody in Washington, I told her.

She said that was crazy; that she was coming. Then I told her that I looked so awful. Worse than she could imagine, I told her. But the last thing she said, before our three minutes were up, was that she was coming.

"What if you aren't in top condition—all prettily shaved and combed?" Ellen asked me in her next letter. "Do you think a wife minds that?

"I have so much to tell you, and this may be my only chance to see you before the baby is born. There are so many, many things dangling in the air that we need to talk over. . . . My condition is no excuse at all.

"Is there still something you haven't told me? I want more than anything in the world to understand you, always. That's why it worries me so, that I can't see through your wanting me to stay here where I'm not needed, when I could be with you."

Ellen's mother wrote me a wonderful letter after that. She told me how Ellen had taken the news and that one of the first things she said was that she was glad the baby was coming.

"You must know how deeply we regret that this should have happened to you," Ellen's mother wrote, "but we know how you'd hate a fuss or pity. You'll never get it from any of us. Because I have had to drag a half-dead leg through life I can offer a little understanding. There will be a lot of things you can't do, but a lot more you can. And there's an extra joy of achievement, love and a peace within.

"It has been so good to have Ellen at home for awhile. She seems to be in an excellent physical condition. While her condition is now apparent, she hasn't lost her daintiness. She has been careful to buy clothes that make her look well-groomed and dignified. I was looking forward to having her where I could share in all the preparations for your baby, but if you can have her with you, that joy belongs to you, and there's no joy or mystery in life equal to that of the first-born.

"Ellen is all packed and ready to come. I don't believe it will harm her physically. Yet if you think it would save you, or be safer for her not to come, I know she will abide by your wishes. And you know we'll be very glad to make the waiting as happy and easy as possible."

I was sitting in my room a day or two later, looking out the window and thinking of her and what would become of us, when the door opened and she stood there. I had tried to kid myself into believing that she'd come across the country on a train, but I should have known Doolittle better than that. Ellen flew, of course. He saw to that.

I had thought so many times of what I'd say and what I'd do, but now all I could think was that Ellen was there, there in my room. Nothing mattered except that.

I jumped up to go to the door, forgetting everything. Forgetting the crutches. And when I took a step toward her I fell on my face in front of her.

The Army doctors went to work on me as soon as they fattened me up a little more, and Ellen was settled in Walter Reed's Hostess House.

The second amputation was as bad as the first one. The spinal anesthetic didn't seem to work as well as it worked in China. But they gave me some Sodium Pentothal during the process of the cutting and the beveling of bone, and I went out cold. There was another operation after that on the leg, a trimming job.

The doctors did a great job on my mouth and jaw.

X-rays showed that the shock of going through the windshield had shoved one of my teeth up through my gums into a section of my sinus. They got that out, along with some broken-off nubs left in the gums, then went to work on the job of reshaping my mouth and chin. Neither had healed straight.

A number of internes—nice fellows I had met around the place—came to watch this one. It was very interesting, though the doctors blindfolded me this time. They marked off sections of scar-tissue to be cut out and places where they'd have to take a kind of hem. They cut these marks with very sharp instruments before giving me novocaine, for novocaine relaxes the muscles in such a way that there would be no way of telling whether they were cutting correctly, if the cutting didn't begin until after the sagging effects of the drug had set in.

"This will hurt you," one of the doctors said, as he cut down through the vermilion border of my lower lip. He wasn't kidding. I could hear the happy internes saying, "Wheel him around this way, so we can see." I tried to say something to them about being a bloodthirsty bunch of blokes.

It took a long time, cutting, shaping and sewing. The doctors spoke only once. One of them said, "Jesus! He's still got some of that beach sand in there."

We spent all of our days together. It was interesting to read the letters Ellen wrote—the ones she couldn't mail. She thought the raid on the Philippines was "it" for a while. But when the first Tokyo raid was announced, by Tokyo, she knew that that was where I was, even though at first the Japanese identified the planes as just "Allied."

"I don't know whether to feel glad it's over, or what," Ellen wrote, when the news was announced. When I was off my nut a little in China, before the operation, Ellen wrote that she didn't know what was the matter: she couldn't sleep. On what must have been the day my leg came off Ellen heard from the wife of one of the boys that I was okay.

Young King Peter, of Yugoslavia, indirectly broke part of the news to my mother. He visited us in Walter Reed June 26th. Two boys hurt at Pearl Harbor, Lieutenant Wallace Pickard and Private Ramon Carazo, were wheeled in and we formed a line of chairs in front of the democratic young King. There were five of us, including McClure and Watson. The King said he was proud of us and shook hands.

The heavily censored story and the pictures were released and turned out to be the first news that anybody had been hurt on the raid. My mother's nurse kept it secret, but my mother found out. She happened to listen to a news broadcast about it, but, surprisingly, it wasn't as much of a blow as we had thought it would be. She knew plenty about me, I learned much later, though the nurse kept all hospital pictures of me away from her.

Twenty-five of the boys were decorated at Bolling Field in a fine ceremony on the 27th. General Arnold and General Doolittle were there to pin the DFC on them. I asked Ellen to go with the other wives to see it, and she did. We had a lot of clips about the boys to paste in our scrapbook, and a lot of the boys came out to the hospital and sat around with us.

Sessler and Parker joined us at the hospital after that, to be treated for their malarial fever, and all of us got our DFC on July 6th. McClure and Watson, with their arms held out from their bodies by casts and braces, and I, sat in pajamas and bathrobes. Doolittle was there, with that infectious grin of his, and so were Major General Millard F. Harmon, chief of the air staff of the Army Air Forces, Secretary of Treasury Morgenthau, Watson's mother, wife and father, McClure's mother and Ellen.

A couple of weeks later, Watson and I got our Captaincies and McClure became a First Lieutenant. Everybody on the raid was jumped one rank, at Doolittle's recommendation. All of us got the Order of the

Purple Heart. Also we were awarded the Military Order of China on July 25th by Major General Chu Shih-ming, Military Attaché at the Chinese Embassy in Washington. Doolittle showed up for that one, too. He was spending a lot of time with us, and it made us all proud as the devil.

The long wait for the baby and for my leg and mouth to get well was hastened along because I could see and talk to Ellen. There were letters to read and write, too. Sergeant Lovelace, who painted the prophetic Ruptured Duck and crossed crutches which, according to a *Gripsholm* evacuee, is on display in a Tokyo square, wrote me to say how bad he felt about missing the raid. The night before we left Eglin Field for the Coast, Lovelace went to town. He hitchhiked a ride coming back to the Field. The car turned over, broke his back and he spent the rest of 1942 in a hospital.

Lovelace tried to make me feel good about the Ruptured Duck. "Personally, I think that damn old crate was a jinx from the start," he wrote. It wasn't. It was a good ship.

Ellen and I heard from Gray quite frequently, and wrote to our "bridesmaid" a lot. What a wonderful, light-hearted fellow Bob was! "I've stopped drinking," he wrote in August from Dinjan. "It's easier to guzzle it. I've led seventeen raids over Burma and got to China once, in a B-25. I flew the P-40 on a strafing mission and re-con missions. I'm down to 170—a mere shadow. I'd like to come home, but why beef? We're short-handed over here. Would you please order a chocolate malted and a bottle of beer and drink them for me even if it kills you?"

A month later Bob wrote, "I've got Shorty Manch for a co-pilot now. We're having a little fun now and then. We've heard so many rumors about what all the fellows got when they got home I wish you'd give me a little cold dope. Manch is still a Second Lieutenant, and I'm still a first. Tell the Little General that every-time we're recommended for promotion over here somebody says, 'They're on detached service, so we can't promote them.' Wish I was going to be there for your one-year anniversary next month."

In his next letter Bob asked us to buy him a small American flag, for he needed it to identify himself in some of the places he was going.

"I have a hunch we'll be home by Xmas," he wrote on October 16th. "There are only eighteen of the old gang left over here. That won't break the Treasury, bringing us home.

"I got my capt. today. It was dated Aug. 21. I sure was tickled because there are fellows coming out of the

States six and eight months behind me who are capts. Sorry I don't know anything about Keith. Will you tell Dory I don't?"

Bob was killed two days after he wrote this letter. And poor Clever, who was hurt so badly in our crash, but pulled through, was killed a month later in a crash near Versailles, Ohio.

In the late Summer of 1942, Ellen found a little furnished apartment pretty close to the Hospital. When her time got close I was able to spend the evenings there with her. I was glad it worked out that way. On the evening of September 25th we were sitting around and talking when she suddenly said that she felt faint. I clumped down the hall of the apartment house on my crutches, calling for someone.

With the help of a kind neighbor I got Ellen to our car. We made it to Walter Reed just in time. Ellen came through it swell. Our little Ann is a sweet baby. She's been a world of joy to us.

McClure and Watson are coming alone fine. I'm coming along all right, too. There was a nerve about as big around as a nickel extending down to the bottom of the stump, but the doctors have killed that off pretty much by injections of alcohol and soft hammering.

Some people have asked me if I find myself getting bitter. It's just the opposite. I'm proud, honest. One of the boys at the Hospital, very upset over an operation which was done at a little post, and which put him in Walter Reed for a long time, told me one day that the Medical Corps had ruled, after a study of my case, that there must be a changed technique in leg amputations. The bone must be beveled the first time, and enough skin must be left to flap over and be sewn to the back of the leg instead of sewn across the bottom where the stump fits into the new leg.

But I feel that if my case proved the value of all that—why, that's okay. I think Doc White did a wonderful job on me, when you think of the handicaps under which he had to work. He saved my life and got me back. That's all anybody could ask for.

Before Doolittle flew to Africa, where he has some of our old gang flying for him, he dropped by the Hospital to say good-bye. He asked me what I wanted more than anything else.

That's how I got around to telling him, for the first time, that what I always wanted to be was an aeronautical engineer.

Postscript

The War Department's official communiqué, giving a full picture of the scope of the raid, was not released until 9:30 P.M. (EWT), April 20, 1943. It follows:

Additional details regarding the raid of 18 April 1942 now may be disclosed.

The USS *Hornet* was the "Shangri-La" from which the American planes took off to bomb military objectives in Tokyo and four other Japanese cities. This aircraft carrier, which carried the flyers of the Army Air Forces to within 800 miles of Tokyo on their mission, subsequently was announced as lost in the Battle of Santa Cruz on 26 Oct. 1942.

The objective of the sixteen North American B-25 medium bombers was to attack definite selected points—armament plants, dock yards, railroad yards and oil refineries—in Tokyo, Yokohama, Nagoya, Kobe, and Osaka. This objective was carried out with accuracy and complete success. At the same time, the raid resulted in freezing within Japan, Nipponese airplanes and other forces which might have been used in offensive operations elsewhere.

The American planes were to have sought specified landing fields in China. Because of a combination of circumstances the planes were unable to reach their assigned landing fields. One came down in Soviet Russian territory. The others made forced or crash landings in China—some in Japanese occupied territory—or in water off the Chinese coast. All these planes were wrecked.

The preparation for the raid on Japan, first conceived in January, 1942, was carried out in the utmost secrecy with thoroughness extending to the most minute details. Maj. Gen. James H. Doolittle, who was then a Lieutenant Colonel and a celebrated flyer, combining the reputations of a dare-devil and a most proficient painstaking technician, chose the men to accompany him on the venture. All were volunteers who at first knew only that they were going on a mission whose importance was equalled only by the hazards involved.

About three months were spent in preparations. General Doolittle and his men finished their training at Eglin Field, Fla. It was the first time that medium bombers of the Army were to take off in numbers from an aircraft carrier of the Navy. Special experience was required.

Using white lines on the field to measure, the flyers concentrated on taking off in the shortest possible distance. Patiently the members of each airplane crew pored over maps, and by pictures and silhouettes learned to recognize instantaneously the features of the course they were to travel over Japan and the particular objectives they were to bomb. The Norden bombsight was replaced with a simple 20-cent sight devised by Capt. (now Maj.) C. R. Greening in order to preserve the secret of the Norden sight should any aircraft be forced down in Japan.

Each plane was given the particular factory or shipyard, or arsenal, or oil works which it was to destroy,—all military targets. At the outset of the training period it was decided that the planes should come in over Japan flying extremely low to escape observation and antiaircraft fire and to make even more sure of the accuracy of their bombing. In practice for the great venture ahead, the planes in training swept in over the American coast and fanned out as they would have to do over Japan to attack their military objectives in or near the five cities which were involved. Exactly similar geographical distances were traveled over American territory toward objectives resembling the goals in Japan.

At a rendezvous port the flyers and their planes were loaded on the aircraft carrier *Hornet* to start the voyage which was to take them within range of Tokyo. The commander of the task force was Admiral William F. Halsey, Jr., who had already achieved fame as a skillful and bold leader of Naval raids upon Japanese bases in the Pacific. Admiral Halsey is now commander of all American Naval and Army forces in the South Pacific area.

Aboard the *Hornet* training was continued. There were lectures on Japan and talks on navigation, gunnery and meteorology. The gunners practiced with shots at kites which were flown above the aircraft carrier.

The original plan was to proceed through hazardous waters to a point within 400 miles of Tokyo. There the planes were to be launched and their fate left to the hands of their crews and to Providence, while the Naval task force made its own precarious escape.

It had been planned to take off just before dark, to make the attack on Japan at night and to arrive at Chinese airfields in the early morning. But when the aircraft carrier was still 800 miles from Tokyo, it met complications. Having avoided one enemy patrol vessel and while trying to steer clear of another, it ran into a third Japanese ship. This ship was sunk, but it was feared at the time that the Japanese aboard it might have been able to use their radio and to warn Tokyo. (It later appeared that this was not the case.) Therefore, instead of waiting until evening and drawing much closer to Japan in the meantime, the planes took off on the morning of 18 April. That was 10 hours ahead of the planned departure time. The added distance to be flown naturally added greatly to the hazards of the mission. But there was not the slightest hesitation. General Doolittle and his men were eager to take off. Whatever the chance of arriving at the airfields in China, they had at least reached a point where Tokyo and other Japanese cities were within bombing distance.

It was agreed that if the planes could not reach the Chinese coast, the men would try the dangerous feat of landing on the water, there to take to their rubber boats.

It was rough weather as General Doolittle bade goodbye to Admiral Halsey and undertook the great adventure. One by one the big Army bombers roared from the aircraft carrier. The take-offs were difficult on a bobbing and slanting deck. Water slapped over the bow of the carrier and planes had to take off on the upbeat. The plane piloted by Lt. Travis Hoover was thrown in such a way that it threatened to fall off on a wing, but Hoover's good piloting saved it.

The first take-off was at 8:20 A.M., ship time, with

General Doolittle piloting the lead plane. It was at 9:20 P.M. that the General was to bail out over China, the last to leave his plane. Much happened in the interval.

The planes wheeled in the sky and headed toward Japan. It was fairly good flying weather and the sun was bright noon as the flyers discerned the coast line. They came in almost skipping the waves, at fifteen or twenty feet above sea level. The low-level flying bore out expectations. The planes were not spotted until they had almost reached their targets. The Japanese were taken entirely by surprise and the presumed warning from the Japanese patrol vessels had not produced an inkling of the American plan to bomb the targets in Japan.

Lt. Travis Hoover led one flight of planes over the northern part of Tokyo. Capt. David M. Jones led another flight over the central part of the city. Capt. Edward J. York took his flight over the southern part of the city and part of Tokyo Bay. Major Greening led a fourth flight over Kenegawa, Yokohama City, and the Yokasuka Navy Yard. Another flight of planes went south of Tokyo and split up to bomb military installations at Nagoya, Osaka and Kobe.

General Doolittle has told how his plane skimmed the roof tops of Tokyo so low that he could even see the surprised faces of Japanese on the streets. At one point a ball game was in progress and the spectators scurried for cover only after the planes had passed. The Americans climbed to 1500 feet for the actual bombing, lest the explosions otherwise destroy their own planes.

There was some attempt by Japanese pursuit planes to intervene. Maj. Charles R. Greening who piloted one of the planes has told of new type Japanese ships which sought to intercept his plane near Tokyo. Major Greening hugged the ground and even flew under some power lines in the hope that the enemy ships would crash into them. They did not, but Major Greening's plane shot down two of the Jap planes. The Major's objective was a gasoline refinery and storage works. The dropped bombs produced sheets of flame and a terrific explosion that banged the heads of Major Greening and his co-pilot against the top of the cockpit. Nearly 50 miles away they could see flames and smoke to the rear, rising from the gas works.

Lt. Col. John A. Hilger, leading the raid on Nagoya, encountered inaccurate antiaircraft fire, and proceeded to bomb and hit an aircraft works, an oil storage warehouse, an arsenal and barracks.

One by one, each objective of each plane was checked off. Now it was a tank factory, now a shipyard with a cruiser in it, now an airplane plant. The explosions and also the flames from incendiary bombs wrecked steel plants, powder factories, machinery works, railroad yards and sidings, docks, arsenals and oil refineries. Direct hits were made on a new cruiser or battleship under construction.

Planes arriving over Tokyo after the first bombings met heavy antiaircraft fire, but no real damage was done to any of the bombers. Flames and columns of smoke leaping several thousand feet into the air marked the trail of the American planes.

Even though the attack on Kobe came probably an hour after the raid had started on Tokyo, it seemed to be a complete surprise to the people on the streets.

More than 30 Japanese pursuit planes were observed during the raids. They were ineffective at interception and several were shot down.

The antiaircraft fire of the Japanese did little damage. When shooting at one of our airplanes, they shot down one of their own barrage balloons which were flying in small numbers.

By order of General Doolittle, no attack was made on the Japanese Emperor's Palace, although it was in sight of the flyers. It was not a military objective.

It was upon leaving Japan that the most hazardous part of the venture was reached. The scattered airplanes ran into a storm. Their already depleted gasoline reserves were drained further as they bucked the winds. Darkness was coming on and the unfamiliar terrain added to the difficulties. There were no light beacons or landing flares. Unable to go farther, there in the darkness 6,000 to 10,000 feet above a strange land, the great majority of the men bailed out.

Most of the men landed in unoccupied China and made their way to Chungking. But some of them landed in the occupied region. This led to the capture of eight. Others made their way out, with the aid of friendly Chinese. Several of them hid away for an extended period until they could escape to the free territory of China. Two of the men are still entirely unaccounted for.

Seven men were injured in crashes but survived. One was killed. Cpl. Leland D. Faktor's parachute opened but he landed in mountainous territory and may have suffered a secondary fall. He was found dead.

The plane piloted by Captain York bombed Tokyo but had so little gas left that it made for Siberia and landed 40 miles north of Vladivostok. The plane was landed safely and the crew was interned.

The crews of two planes came down close to Japanese positions. They contained the men listed as missing or presumed to be prisoners of war.

Lt. Charles J. Ozuk, navigator on the same plane as Corporal Faktor, was injured, as were Lieutenants

Ted W. Lawson, Dean Davenport, Charles L. Mc-Clure, Robert S. Clever, Harold F. Watson, and Corporal David J. Thatcher. All survived.

In this connection, Corporal Thatcher was cited for his initiative and courage in tending his companions after their plane crashed in the water. This aircraft piloted by Lieutenant Lawson landed in the China Sea with a shock which seriously injured him and the other crew members. Thatcher, although badly cut on the head and momentarily knocked unconscious when the plane hit the sea and turned over, nevertheless swam back to secure the medical kit from the crushed plane. He was the only one physically able to carry it.

After it became plain that any further wait would result in capture by the Japanese forces, which were only about three miles away, Thatcher persuaded Chinese fishermen to carry his injured crew mates to temporary safety around the Japanese outposts. Chinese villagers carried his companions over mountains and difficult terrain until they reached medical aid. All of this plane's crew were saved either from capture or death as a result of Corporal Thatcher's initiative and courage in assuming responsibility and tending the wounds himself day and night, and arranging for the transportation of his companions.

Lt. J. R. White, flight surgeon who flew in the

plane piloted by Lt. Donald G. Smith, also was commended for bravery.

Lieutenant White "at great risk of his life and with exemplary courage" remained inside the sinking plane, with water rising dangerously, until his surgical instruments and medical kit could be salvaged. The plane plunged into 100 feet of water just after he had completed this effort and escaped. Later on, Lieutenant White remained in dangerous territory tending the injuries of the crewmen of Lieutenant Lawson's plane.

The preoccupation in bringing American flyers to safety was a principal reason why no detailed statement was issued after the raid. To have named the flyers and disclosed that they were still missing would have intensified the efforts of the Japanese to capture them. Also, consideration had to be given to the possibility of reprisals on friendly Chinese who helped the Americans in Japanese-occupied China.

The initial secrecy was essential to permit the small Naval task force to elude the Japanese surface vessels which were between the American warships and the outer Pacific. As long as this secrecy could be maintained the Japanese were obliged to set up defenses against a number of possibilities. They could not be sure whether the planes had come from China or an aircraft carrier, or some stepping stone in the

North Pacific. They did not know when the attack might be repeated. Thus, the Japanese were forced to tie up part of their military strength during crucial months.

If the secret could always have been kept from the Japanese—which in the end was impossible—it would naturally have added to the tension with which Japan awaits the attacks that still lie ahead.

The following lists show what happened at the time to those who took part in the raid on Japan. The men and their next of kin are listed.

INTERNED IN RUSSIA

1st Lt. Robert Gabel Emmens—Mrs. J. J. Emmens, mother, 1443 E. Main St., Medford, Ore.

2nd Lt. Nolan A. Herndon—Mrs. J. T. Herndon, mother, Sulphur Springs, Tex.

Sgt. Theodore H. Laban—Mr. Henry J. Laban, father, Kenosha, Wisc.

Cpl. David W. Pohl—Mrs. Martha Pohl, mother, 84 Edgemoor Ave., Wellesley, Mass.

Maj. Edward J. York—Mrs. E. J. York, wife, 28 Kingbridge Oval, San Antonio, Tex. Mrs. I. Chichowski, mother, 104 Harvester Ave., Batavia, N.Y.

MISSING IN ACTION

Sgt. William J. Dieter—Mrs. Jesse T. Dieter, mother, Route 1, Box 222, Tule Lake, Calif.

Cpl. Donald E. Fitzmaurice—Mrs. William F. Fitzmaurice, mother, 4308 Lenox St., Lincoln, Nebr.

PRISONERS OF WAR

2nd Lt. George Barr—Mrs. William Maas, sister, Elizabeth Waters Hall, No. 1403, U. of Wisc., Madison, Wisc.

1st Lt. William Glover Farrow—Mrs. Jessie Farrow, mother, 1619 Varnum St., Washington, D.C.

1st Lt. Robert L. Hite—Mr. Robert P. Hite, father, Earth, Texas.

1st Lt. Robert J. Meder—Mrs. J. J. Meder, mother, 1622 Elmwood Ave., Lakewood, Ohio.

1st Lt. Chase J. Nielson—Mrs. Chase J. Nielson, wife, Box 164, Hyrum, Utah.

PRESUMED TO BE PRISONERS OF WAR

1st Lt. Dean E. Hallmark—Mrs. O. D. Hallmark, mother, 808 Wayne Ave., Dallas, Tex.

Cpl. Jacob D. Deshazer—Mrs. Hulda Andrus, mother, General Delivery, Madras, Ore.

Sgt. Harold A. Spatz—Mr. Robert A. Spatz, father, Lebo, Kans.

KILLED IN ACTION

Cpl. Leland D. Faktor—Mr. Edward Cinkle, uncle, Plymouth, Iowa.

PARTICIPATED IN RAID AND
REACHED SAFETY THEREAFTER

Maj. Gen. James H. Doolittle—Mrs. J. H. Doolittle, wife, 25th & Q Sts., N.W., Washington, D.C.

Maj. John A. Hilger—Virginia B. Hilger, 83 Parkton Road, Jamaica Plain, Mass.

Capt. Charles R. Greening—Mrs. Dorothy W. Greening, wife, 518½ Simpson Ave., Hoquiam, Wash.

Capt. David M. Jones—Mrs. D. M. Jones, wife, Winters, Tex.

Lt. Thadd H. Blanton—Mrs. J. M. Russell, mother, 604 S. Denton St., Gainesville, Tex.

Lt. William M. Bower—Mrs. Kathryn M. Bower, mother, 2826 E. 130th St., Cleveland, Ohio.

Lt. Clayton J. Campbell—Mrs. C. J. Campbell, wife, 420 Michigan Ave., Orofino, Idaho.

Lt. Robert S. Clever, 2116 Southwest Second Ave., Portland, Ore.

Lt. Richard E. Cole—Mrs. Fred Cole, mother, 747 Faulkner Ave., Dayton, Ohio.

Lt. Horace E. Crouch—Mrs. H. E. Crouch, 1611 Marion St., Columbia, S.C.

Lt. Dean Davenport—3444 N. E. Bryce, Portland, Ore.

Lt. William N. Fitzhugh—Mr. J. G. Fitzhugh, 2906 Avenue Q., Galveston, Tex.

Lt. Robert M. Gray—Mr. James M. Gray, father, Box 215, Killeen, Tex.

Lt. Thomas C. Griffin—5417 Maryland Ave., Chicago, Ill.

Lt. Everett W. Holstrom—Mrs. E. W. Holstrom, 3807 N. 39th St., Tacoma, Wash.

Lt. Travis Hoover—2651 Jackson St., Route 2, Arlington, Calif.

Lt. Frank A. Kappeler—Mr. George F. Kappeler, father, 2992 Johnson Ave., Alameda, Calif.

Lt. Richard A. Knobloch—Mr. William F. Knobloch, father, Fort Sheridan, Ill.

Lt. Richard O. Joyce—Mrs. R. M. Joyce, mother, 2455 Ryons St., Lincoln, Neb.

Lt. Ted W. Lawson—2218½ Vineyard, Los Angeles, Calif.

Lt. Charles L. McClure—3 Harvard Ave., University City, Mo.

Lt. Harry C. McCool—Mrs. S. O. McCool, mother, 2520 W. Pike Peak Ave., Colorado Springs, Colo.

Lt. E. E. McElroy—Mrs. E. E. McElroy, wife, 100 Young St., Longview, Tex.

Lt. Eugene McGurl—Mr. and Mrs. Owen McGurl, parents, 18 Grove Pl., Arlington, Mass.

Lt. J. H. Macia—Mrs. J. H. Macia, Jr., 2834 E. 4th St., Tucson, Ariz.

Lt. Jack E. Manch—Mr. and Mrs. M. G. Manch, parents, 223 N. Lewis St., Staunton, Va.

Lt. Richard E. Miller—Mr. Edmund H. Miller, father, 3408 N. Washington Road, Fort Wayne, Ind.

Lt. Charles J. Ozuk—4441 North Elston Ave., Chicago, Ill.

Lt. James M. Parker, Jr.—Box 368, Livingston, Tex.

Lt. Henry A. Potter—Mr. A. R. Potter, 604 W. Pleasant Drive, Pierre, S.D.

Lt. William R. Pound, Jr.—Mrs. Iola M. Pound, wife, 1635 S. Primrose Ave., Alhambra, Calif.

Lt. Kenneth E. Reddy—Mr. J. W. Reddy, father, Box 135, Bowie, Tex.

Lt. Howard A. Sessler—52 Fountain Road, Arlington, Mass.

Lt. Jack A. Sims—902 West Lovell St., Kalamazoo, Mich.

Lt. Donald G. Smith—Belle Fourche, S.D.

Lt. J. Royden Stork—Mrs. W. E. Stork, 3771 Center St., San Diego, Calif.

Lt. Denver N. Truelove—Mrs. Clyde W. Truelove, mother, Box 84, Lula, Ga.

Lt. Harold F. Watson—21 Robin Road, West Hartford, Conn.

Lt. Thomas R. White—520 Sunset Drive, Redlands, Calif.

Lt. Rodney R. Wilder—Mrs. L. A. Wilder, mother, 906 Cecelia St., Taylor, Tex.

Lt. Carl N. Wildner—Belchertown Road, Amherst, Mass.

Lt. Griffith P. Williams—4158 Menlo St., San Diego, Calif.

Lt. Lucian N. Youngblood—Mrs. L'Gean K. Youngblood, wife, 1623 N. 11th St., Waco, Tex.

T. Sgt. Waldo J. Bither—Mrs. W. J. Bither, wife, 432 Wichita St., Shreveport, La.

T. Sgt. Eldred V. Scott—Box 294, R. D. No. 8, Phoenix, Ariz.

S. Sgt. Edwin B. Bain—Mrs. Catherine Bain, 616 5th Ave., Greensboro, N.C.

S. Sgt. William L. Birch—Mrs. W. J. Collison, mother, 222 18th St., Bakersfield, Calif.

S. Sgt. Fred A. Braemer—Mrs. F. A. Braemer, 111½ 12th Ave., North Seattle, Wash.

S. Sgt. Omer A. Duquette—Mr. Sylvio Duquette, brother, 10 Tuckerman St., West Warwick, R.I.

S. Sgt. Jacob Eierman—Mr. J. G. Eierman, 3801 Atlantic Ave., Atlantic City, N.J.

S. Sgt. Edwin W. Horton, Jr.—Mrs. Edwin Horton, Sr., mother, North Eastam, Barnstable, Mass.

S. Sgt. P. J. Leonard—Mrs. P. J. Leonard, wife, 3034 Race St., Denver, Colo.

Sgt. Wayne M. Bissell—Mr. and Mrs. Max E. Bissell, parents, 2214 E. 5th St., Vancouver, Wash.

Sgt. Robert C. Bourgeois—Mrs. R. C. Bourgeois, 3015 Eagle St., New Orleans, La.

Sgt. Melvin J. Gardner—Mrs. Alice Gardner, mother, Linden, Ariz.

Sgt. Aden E. Jones—Mrs. Agnes Stretch, mother, 1831 N. Mareng Ave., Pasadena, Calif.

Sgt. George E. Larkin, Jr.—Mrs. G. E. Larkin, Sr., mother, P.O. Box 83, New Haven, Ky.

Sgt. Joseph W. Manske—Mrs. William G. Manske, mother, 164 Commercial St., Gowanda, N.Y.

S. Sgt. Douglas V. Radney—Mineola, Tex.

Sgt. Edward J. Saylor—Brusett, Mont.

Sgt. Robert J. Stephens—Mrs. E. E. Martin, Rural Route 3, Hobart, Okla.

Corp. David J. Thatcher—Mr. and Mrs. Joseph H. Thatcher, Box 307, R.F.D. No. 1, Billings, Mont.

Sgt. Adam R. Williams—Mrs. W. L. Williams, 216 Randolph St., Morgantown, N.C.

Cpl. Burt M. Jordan—Mrs. Ida I. Jordan, mother, Route No. 1, Covington, Okla.

After One Year

There are many things left to say, now that the story of the raid can be told. The little pieces fit themselves together, the sums add up. We know more about what we did to the Japanese, physically and spiritually, and what they did to us.

A year after the raid, this is our score:

Fifty-five of the eighty men on the raid got back either to action elsewhere or to the United States. Eight were captured, eight remained in China to fly for Major General Claire Chennault. Five were interned in Russia. Two men from the planes of Hallmark and Farrow are declared missing. The Chinese grapevine said they were dead. Corporal Faktor, as I related, was killed outright.

Gray and Clever were killed months before the War Department's release of the story, and have been accounted for earlier. But to these must be added such post-raid casualties as Gene McGurl and Sergeant Melvin Gardner, who never came back from an attack on the Burma Road in June, 1942—a raid which also cost us Staff Sergeant Omer Duquette. It must have been the first raid these three fellows engaged in after Generalissimo Chiang Kai-shek gave the boys a state banquet when they finally assembled in Chungking.

Ken Reddy was killed in a crash in Little Rock, Arkansas, September 3, 1942—after all he had been through. It was just a routine flight, such as the one that claimed poor Clever. Dick Miller got it in North Africa in January, 1943, as did Staff Sergeant P. J. Leonard. Don Smith, whose water landing near Nantien saved my life after the raid, because Doc White was aboard Don's B-25, was killed over Europe in November, 1942. Davey Jones was forced down in Tunisia and has written me from a German prison camp.

These are awful anti-climaxes, God knows, but I believe that if any of us on the raid had our choice of death in action or capture by the Japanese everyone would rather take a chance on death. If the Ruptured Duck had been hit badly by anti-aircraft or enemy plane action over Tokyo I would have dived it, and us, into the likeliest-looking target. The boys in my plane knew this. Others would have done the same thing.

It's hard to write about the boys the Japanese caught in China and took back to Tokyo. There is little to add to what the President said, the day after the full communiqué on the raid was released:

"It is with a feeling of deepest horror, which I know will be shared by all civilized peoples, that I have to announce the barbarous execution by the Japanese Government of some of the members of this country's armed forces who fell into Japanese hands as an incident of warfare."

The President said that this Government had learned of the "trials" of our men by way of the Japanese radio on October 19, 1942. More details were sought immediately by our State Department through the representatives of the neutral Swiss Government in Tokyo. But we got no reply until the following March 12th, and then the Japs answered that the death sentence had been formally pronounced on all the men caught. But "in some cases" it had been commuted. The Japs wouldn't give the names of the men they murdered or the men they spared—if "spared" is the word for what must be a lot worse than death.

Some time after the middle of April, 1943, the State Department also learned that those boys who had not been put to death were "not being treated as prisoners of war." The Swiss Minister to Tokyo was not permitted to visit our men. The same Japanese note also said that we had intentionally bombed non-military installations and had deliberately fired on civilians. It said that the captured fliers had admitted these facts.

You know what a damned lie that is. All but four of the bombs our bunch dropped were aimed at military objectives from what amounted to point-blank range. We checked each other carefully by personal contact or mail during the year that followed the raid, and the only bombing plan that went amiss was that Brick Holstrom had to jettison his four bombs into the water when his ship's guns jammed during a running battle with a pack of Zeros.

We knew before we took off the deck of the *Hornet* that no matter how carefully we bombed we'd be accused of hitting the usual churches and hospitals. It made us that much more careful. Reports that have trickled out of Japan since the raid indicate that many of the people who died that Saturday afternoon were victims of an absence of proper air-raid shelters. If we had been out after anything except machinery we could have bombed the Palace to splinters or destroyed as many schools, shrines and hospitals as we had bombs. Our targets were so indelibly in our minds that we even dreamed about hitting them. You'll remember that I even passed up an anchored aircraft carrier to get to mine, and so did others whose assignment was Tokyo.

As for the "confessions" of our boys, you can be certain that they were made up in the heads of the

Japanese jail keepers, though it makes me sick to specu-
late on what the devils might have done to try to torture
it out of our fellows. The Japs are just as Lieutenant
Commander Jurika told us on the *Hornet*—"inhuman."

The clearest account of what it was like in the
streets of Tokyo that day of the raid came from Ramon
Muniz Lavalle, former commercial attaché of the Ar-
gentine Embassy in Tokyo. Lavalle had gone to Tokyo
around the first of April, 1942. He had worked for four
months in Hong Kong, after the Japs took the place.
His Government was at that time more or less friendly
with Japan, but Lavalle learned enough at Hong Kong
to turn him away from his Government's service. He
had documented proof that the Japs bayonetted
wounded British soldiers in their Stanley Hospital beds,
and he himself saw British women, with their hands
tied behind them, thrown on the streets and raped re-
peatedly by looting Japanese soldiers.

Lavalle was at work in his embassy the day we
came over. He said, when he finally got back to this
country to work for OWI, that he was surprised to hear
an air-raid alarm in Tokyo that day because he himself
was beginning to share the Japanese belief and official
boast that their cities could never be bombed.

"I ran up to our roof and saw four American

bombers flying in over the rooftops," he related. "They couldn't have been more than 100 feet off the ground. I looked down the streets. All Tokyo seemed to be in panic. Japs were running everywhere, pushing, shouting, screaming. There were no air-raid shelters in the city. There still aren't any. Japanese homes have no cellars or basements. I could see fires starting near the port.

"Our two Japanese interpreters in the embassy were frightened out of their skins. I sent down to get them, but they wouldn't come up to the roof. After a raid, a Japanese scrubwoman who worked for us came up to me and said, 'If these raids go on, we'll all go mad.'

"That raid by Doolittle was one of the greatest psychological tricks ever used. It caught the Japs by surprise. Their unbounded confidence began to crack.

"The day after the raid, the Tokyo newspapers said nine American planes had been shot down. I didn't even see nine American planes over Tokyo. The people knew such a statement was a lie. [Note: There were only seven on the Tokyo mission. The Ruptured Duck was next to last to fly over.] The officer in charge of the Japanese anti-aircraft defenses was compelled to commit suicide. I know for a fact that the anti-aircraft force was removed.

"The results of the Doolittle raid are still evident in Japan. They are stamped into the daily living habits of the Japanese people. Where before they imagined themselves safe from aerial aggression, they now search the skies each morning and each night.

"The Japanese newspapers carry pictures of American planes and say these planes are practicing in Texas on how to bomb Tokyo. Fire brigades have been organized. Fire drills are practiced. Fearlessness has turned to fear."

Right after the War Department's delayed raid communiqué, the Japanese radio beamed what it called a warning to future raiders. It mentioned the execution of "some of Doolittle's companions," and said, "This same policy will continue to be enforced in the future. And by the way, don't forget, America," the English-language broadcast added, "make sure that every flier that comes here has a special pass to hell, and rest assured it's strictly a one-way ticket."

As if that would stop our air forces when the time comes to follow up our jab with an overhand right.

As great a shock as it was to hear about the execution of some of our fellows and the probable torture of others, it was equally hard to take the eventual news from the Generalissimo that the Japs had systematically slaughtered all Chinese who helped us after our crashes. We may never know how systematic they really were; how many of those who actually helped us did, in fact, get caught. But the Japs must have been thorough, and pitiless. There can't be any parallel in history for the ruthlessness the Japs have shown to the Chinese during the six years of their war. Madame Chiang Kai-shek wrote not long ago that during the entire span of the war that began for China in 1937 the Japanese have not taken one Chinese prisoner.

That fact would be the gruesome answer to a natural question as to whether some of those who helped us and were caught had been shown even as much mercy as a long prison sentence or a short period of torture before death. They must have been dealt with as horribly as possible, as a warning to Chinese who might be thinking of helping other American aviators who, inevitably, will land in China in the series of future raids which, I pray, will blow Japan off the map of the world.

I keep thinking of those brave, tireless and loyal men and women who picked us up, carried us on their backs, fed us, nursed us back to health and got us away. And I wonder if their knowledge that some of those whom they thus saved would come back to bomb again and again was any comfort to them when they were dragged off to their deaths.

There isn't any way to moralize about those innocent Chinese who must have been put to death on the charge of helping us though they perhaps never heard of us, or the raid, but simply happened to be in the neighborhood when the Japs came along our escape trails to wipe out the very memory of us. What can you say?

But, as painstakingly merciless as Japs are, they must have missed some of those who gave us comfort and a hope of escape. That is the reason why certain names have been changed in this book and why some of the names of Chinese villages have been disguised.

I keep thinking about Charlie, hoping he's still alive—and then wondering how many he carried with him if they finally cornered him. Charlie will fight them until he has nothing left but his teeth. Charlie is the heart of China.

The *Hornet*'s ending must have been beyond description. She went to the bottom during the battle of Santa Cruz, early that following fall, when seemingly every plane in the Japanese air armada concentrated on her. As can be well imagined, she put up a fearful battle, but the Japs were out to sink her at any cost. They knew what the *Hornet* had done, and how well. They threw everything they had against her: high-level bombs, dive bombers and suicidal torpedo bombers.

Months had been spent searching for her. They called her the "Blue Ghost."

She was a great ship, manned by the kind of men who would come back fighting after such disheartening losses as twenty-nine out of the thirty men in Torpedo Bombing Squadron 8. That happened at the Battle of Midway in an attack on a Japanese carrier. The *Hornet* helped to save not only Midway but Hawaii. She was just as great in the late summer fighting in the Solomons.

The *Hornet* must have taken even that final dive with inherent class.

There are a few personal things to add. They round out the story I've told earlier.

My mother died January 16, 1943, from the effects of her stroke. I was still being treated at Walter Reed, but the Army let me go to the Coast for the funeral. The new leg didn't fit especially well. There was a dip in it that gave me trouble, even with a cane. But it worked well enough. I got out to the Coast by bomber and transport plane, getting lifts where I could find them.

Friends on the Coast were very decent about the leg. They didn't keep helping me, but I was relieved whenever I thought this: If my mother had to go, that she went without really knowing I had lost it. I didn't want her to know the whole story until the day when I could walk in on her as if nothing had happened to me.

But the day after the funeral, as I was going through some of my mother's personal papers, I learned with a real shock that she knew—she knew all along that I had lost it. She never let on to me that she knew. I guess she thought it was better that way, and let me continue to wire cheerfully to her about my condition. She wanted *me* to keep from worry, from the worry of wondering how badly the news had affected her.

My mother actually learned about my leg in a letter from Mr. Parker, the missionary, written after the Chinese carried us away from the little village hospital where my leg had been taken. Mrs. Parker enclosed another letter with her husband's note to my mother.

I had believed for all these months that no mail that concerned our injuries or the crash of our planes had been permitted to leave Chungking. The news had to be kept from the Japanese, and men still missing between the China coast and Chungking had to be given a chance to reach the capital or some other safe haven.

But the missionaries' letters got out, somehow, and they reached my mother at a time when I was writing her that I felt great and would be walking in on her one of these days. I am taking the liberty of reproducing them here, together with three letters from Chinese friends.

These letters bring back all the wordless gratitude I have for what these people did for me, and all the terrible helplessness of knowing that now there is nothing I can do in return.

T.W.L.

Letters

A Normal School Somewhere in China
April 30, 1942

Gentlemen:

With great delight I learn that you bombed Japanese great cities as Tokyo, Kobe, and Nagoya. How hard your work is! How brave you are! How brilliant you achieve a victory! I admire you and most honor you. The eyes of the world have been focused on you, looking for fruitful results of your important mission of bombing Japan.

We know the results of bombing Japanese great cities make all the peace-like people obtain a hope of complete victory and also make Japanese people feel that they have been deceived under the empty victory by their war lord. It is also a sign that the Allies begin to fight an offensive war on all battle-front of the world.

We are not a war-like people. We are not interested in aggression. We do not covet one square inch of the territory of any other nation. But we have to bomb Japan in winning this most brutal, most terrible of all wars for the maintenance of Democracy.

Bomb Japan! Bomb Japan! We destroy their trans-
portations industries and military preparations. We
break down the Japanese war-makers' dream of a huge
Asiatic empire. Then our allies will conquer the axis
powers in the near future. Then the welfare of
mankind may be perpetuated.

You will be heroes of many victories. I hope you
recover your health and bomb Japan again.

Yours truely
Shino

District Court
Chekiang, China
April 22, 1942

Dear Cap. Lawson and Aviators From America:

Fortunately I have the opportunity to write to you
as you take this long flight across the Pacific Ocean to
our country especially during the present.

I warmly Greet you in the name of our people and
assure you our deepest concern and respects in your
bravery and vigorousness because you fight against
Fascism and rampant aggression for the Justice and
Liberty of the world in spite of all dangers.

Really our people were very cheerful and happy
for your passing through our city last week. But I am so
sorry that the inconvenience of the communications

which are influenced by war Keep us from supplying you fine foods and medicines.

Now I represent the people of the whole district about 160,000 populations to give our best wishes to you that you will be recovered easily and will help us to win the final victory.

Don't forget the name of our city. That you have visited.

Respectfully yours Kai-san
The Magistrate

Mission House
Chekiang
China, May 31, 1942

Dear Mrs. Lawson,

I have been asked by your son, Lieutenant Lawson, to write to you. The few weeks he was here among us went by so quickly, yet they were full of many anxious moments, for when he reached this town he was very ill. One night we despaired of his life, then six of us missionaries held a prayer meeting on his behalf, asking God to spare him. From that time on he began to improve. Just before your son left us, I reminded him that he was alive in answer to prayer. We all share the joy of his recovery. When he was very ill, he asked me to be with him. He was too ill to speak much, so I used to read to him from the Bible well-known scriptures which he remembered having heard before. Then I knelt in prayer, committing him to God. He did enjoy these times, and often spoke of you and of your prayers for him. Almost the first thing I heard him say when he reached here was that he had a praying mother. Your prayers have been answered; your dear son is now regaining health and strength again, and, best of all, I believe he has come to know God in a new and deeper way through his suffering.

All the men of his crew were fond of your son, and affectionately called him "Ted." They all were good men, and we thank God that we ever came into contact with them. Now they have left us, starting on a long journey to the Chinese capital. I hope you will soon have the joy of seeing your dear son soon home. You will be distressed to see him as he is, yet try to think of the great mercy of God in sparing his life. I trust God has preserved him for a great purpose, and though we most likely will not see him again, yet often we will uphold him in our prayers. We cannot always understand God's ways with us and our loved ones, yet we trust Him, for He gave His own dear Son to die for us. No more now. May God bless you and your dear son, Lieutenant Lawson, is the prayer of,

Yours sincerely,
George Parker

30-5-42

Dear Mrs. Lawson,

You will be surprised to hear from an utter
stranger, but when I tell you we write at the request of
your son, you will pardon the intrusion. We had the
privilege of having Lieutenant Lawson and his crew in
our city for four weeks, and, when he left for Chungking, he asked us to write to you. The plane he was
flying had to make a forced landing on the Chekiang
coast, and in the smash all the men were injured to
some extent. Unfortunately, medical aid was not available immediately, with the result that by the time the
men reached the hospital here, their wounds were
septic, after four days' inadequate care. Two Chinese
doctors here, both trained by British doctors, gave
every care to the wounded men, and our small com-
munity of four missionaries did what we could by inter-
preting, etc., but we were all much relieved when Dr.
White of the Air Force arrived three days after the first
crew. His plane had also been wrecked but none
injured, so the rest of his crew went on, but the doctor
stayed to care for the wounded and traveled with them
across China. We felt it was a definite answer to your
prayers that the doctor should be in the only other
plane that came this way.

But you want more details of your brave boy, who

endeared himself to us all in those weeks here when his sufferings were often great. For two weeks the doctors fought hard to save Lieutenant Lawson's left leg, but it became evident it would be dangerous to delay amputating it, and with deep regret Dr. White removed his left leg above the knee. Dear Mrs. Lawson, I know this is going to be a bad blow for you, but the mother of such a son must be a brave woman, and we do pray that God will sustain and comfort you in this new trial. Quite frankly, it is a miracle your boy is alive and the loss of his leg is a small matter compared with what might so easily have been. He had other wounds, face and arm, but these were healing well when he left us. Dr. White going with them was a great comfort to us all as it ensured expert care.

Some of the other men were badly wounded too, but they were all so brave. It was a real privilege to be able to do anything for them, even in a small way. An American nurse, also a member of our Mission, came with her husband and two children from a neighboring city to help, and she spent most of her time caring for Lieutenant Lawson. It was remarkable he should come here where such help was available as nowhere else in this province could he have had it. Surely God made provision for the dear boys' needs.

It is almost two weeks since they left us and we

have not heard how they are, but feel sure they are being well cared for, as the Chinese Government and people were very kind to them all the way. I do hope you will soon have your son home with you for his long convalescence to perfect health. I wonder if I dare ask you to write to us, just once, to let us know of his return home and condition? We would be so grateful if you can do this, for we've all grown to love "Ted." He talked so much about you, you don't seem a stranger! Trust this will not be too great a shock for your daughter-in-law. My husband is adding a note, so I need say no more.

With kindest regards,
I remain,
Sincerely yours,
Alice Parker

P.S. An expected Japanese occupation of this place has delayed this letter, but I trust it gets out all right.

United States Atlantic Fleet
Eighth Fleet
29 March 1946

Capt. Ted W. Lawson
5402 Brada
Los Angeles, Calif.

Dear Captain Lawson:

On April 18, 1942, the first blow against the Japanese homeland was struck by American planes, jumping off from an undisclosed point to bomb Tokyo. To Americans, grimly facing reverses on every front, it brought an electric shock of hope. To an arrogant enemy, it foreshadowed inevitable defeat.

A folder of photographs depicting the dramatic operation has been prepared by the United States Navy especially for the surviving members of the "Shangri-La" team and for the families of their comrades whose lives were lost. I have attached a copy, which I know you will treasure.

As commanding officer of the U.S.S. HORNET at the time the raid was launched from her decks, I share your pride in the skill and daring of the men who flew with "Jimmy" Doolittle on that mission.

In behalf of the Naval Service, I extend warmest regards.

Sincerely,
M. A. Mitscher,
Admiral, U.S. Navy

Admiral M. A. MITSCHER, U.S.N.,
Commander EIGHTH Fleet,
c/o Fleet Post Office,
New York, N.Y.